PEN

A TA

Born in 1948 to a Brahmin and a Shia Muslim mother, Mahesh Bhatt, in a career spanning almost four decades, has rewritten several rules and thereafter broken most of them. He began his journey in the film industry with *Manzilein Aur Bhi Hain* in 1973. He then broke new ground with *Arth* which received critical and commercial acclaim. He followed *Arth* with *Saransh*, *Janam*, *Daddy*, *Sir*, *Tamanna* and, finally, the National Award-winning *Zakhm*. Today he does not direct films but is still involved in the film industry and has written screenplays for movies such as *Raaz*, *Jism*, *Murder*, *Zeher*, *Kalyug* and *Gangster*. He has also directed several documentaries and has anchored and hosted for Sahara Television *Haqueeqat*, a show on human right violations, as well as *Imaging Science*, a show telecast on Doordarshan.

Mahesh Bhatt wrote *U.G. Krishnamurti: A Life* which has been translated into several languages. He contributes regularly to newspapers of national circulation in English (*Times of India*, *Indian Express*, *Hindustan Times*, *Pioneer*, *The Hindu* and others) as well as in Hindi (*Dainik Jagran* and *Dainik Bhaskar*). He also compiled, edited and wrote the foreword for a book of quotations of U.G. Krishnamurti called *The Little Book of Questions*.

PENGUIN BOOKS

A TASTE OF LIFE

Born in 1948 to a Hindu father and a ... Muslim mother ... [illegible]

A Taste of Life

The Last Days of U.G. Krishnamurti

Mahesh Bhatt

PENGUIN BOOKS

PENGUIN BOOKS
Published by the Penguin Group
Penguin Books India Pvt. Ltd, 7th Floor, Infinity Tower C, DLF Cyber City, Gurgaon 122 002, Haryana, India
Penguin Group (USA) Inc., 375 Hudson Street, New York, New York 10014, USA
Penguin Group (Canada), 90 Eglinton Avenue East, Suite 700, Toronto, Ontario, M4P 2Y3, Canada
Penguin Books Ltd, 80 Strand, London WC2R 0RL, England
Penguin Ireland, 25 St Stephen's Green, Dublin 2, Ireland (a division of Penguin Books Ltd)
Penguin Group (Australia), 707 Collins Street, Melbourne, Victoria 3008, Australia
Penguin Group (NZ), 67 Apollo Drive, Rosedale, Auckland 0632, New Zealand
Penguin Books (South Africa) (Pty) Ltd, Block D, Rosebank Office Park, 181 Jan Smuts Avenue, Parktown North, Johannesburg 2193, South Africa

Penguin Books Ltd, Registered Offices: 80 Strand, London WC2R 0RL, England

First published by Penguin Books India 2009

10 9 8 7 6 5 4 3

ISBN 9780143067160

Typeset in Dante MT by SŪRYA, New Delhi
Printed at Repro India Ltd, Navi Mumbai

A PENGUIN RANDOM HOUSE COMPANY

To Larry and Susan, who helped me make it through the long night and my wife Soni, who helped me put into words those feelings which only the heart can hear.

Contents

Prologue

At about quarter past eight on the morning of 22 March 2007, Susan screamed, 'Oh my god, Mahesh, look, ants!' I turned and saw thousands of black ants marching in line on the white carpet, up the white sofa and on to U.G.'s stone-like face where they spread out and completely darkened the left side. We moved closer and saw that there were thousands, moving with the frantic intensity of life, in contrast to U.G.'s utter calm. I shouted to Larry to come help us. I remembered that someone had once asked U.G. what the ants were doing in his room. He had replied, 'They're coming for me.'

We used a repellent and with great effort managed to drive the ants away. Susan had bought the eco-friendly spray only the other day and little did we know that it would be put to use so soon and that too for such a bizarre task. Susan then used her doctor's dexterity to change U.G.'s sheets with Larry and me assisting. The question that bothered us was how the insects went straight to U.G. with all of us keeping watch. Larry said that he too had been bothered by the ants when he was meditating in the room; maybe the ants only approached when one was absolutely still. I was reminded of U.G.'s prophetic words: 'Unless man comes to terms with the fact that he is no more significant than the mosquito or the ant, he is doomed.'

By midday, I began to feel restless. I walked up to the tiny fridge and opened it. It was bare except for a golden box of Leonidas chocolates with four pieces in it. I offered them to Susan and Larry; they took one each. I turned to U.G. and said, 'Happy death day, U.G.,' before popping the chocolates into my mouth. As I ate, it struck me that U.G.'s death saga had turned into a kind of black comedy which he himself had orchestrated.

In the afternoon, Susan suggested that we should go away for a while and give U.G. a chance to make his exit. By 2.30 p.m., Larry and Susan were in the garden, calling me out to join them. Everything was still. I walked towards the door and turned. My master was clearly alive and breathing. I bent down and touched his feet; they were coated with flakes of dry, ash-like skin. I felt my pulse throb in my fingers but hardly any life in those toes with which I had such friendship. I gazed at him affectionately and said to him, 'U.G., I'm going out so that you can go away. I want to thank you for all that you have done for me in case I don't find you here on my return.' Something in that very explosive silence told me that my words had reached him in some subliminal way. I bent down, kissed his feet and made a brave attempt to go out but couldn't. I am me; U.G. could walk away from things and never look back but I can't. So I turned back and looked at him, inhaling the moment deeply; it was the only point in time I would retain with me and forever find sustenance from. I left, feeling strangely like I was walking away yet was somehow standing next to U.G. My cellphone beeped, it was an SMS from Vishesh, my nephew: 'Please thank U.G. on my behalf. I have no words to express the importance of meeting him in my life.'

Susan, Larry and I wandered the lazy, deserted afternoon streets of Vallecrosia. We stepped into a departmental store and tried to figure out if anyone needed anything but soon realized that this was only one of our excuses to stay away from the villa. We then walked into a coffee bar to have a cappuccino. An Italian soap opera was playing on television and the coffee bar was deserted. Susan was feeling guilty about leaving U.G. unattended. I told her that we were doing the right thing; that we had chosen to give U.G. a chance to go away. She calmed down slightly.

In spite of all our efforts, we soon headed back. We walked through the gate and the three of us were doing all we could to keep ourselves from rushing into the villa. The time on my cellphone was 3.08 p.m. Larry finally decided to step in to check and disappeared for some time. Susan turned to me and stared. Then we heard Larry's voice, 'He has stopped breathing.' We entered, pretending that everything was under control; that everything was as it should be. We found U.G. exactly the way we had left him. My old man had kept his pact. I was the only person he wanted to see in his final moments and that was how it happened.

Uppaluri Gopala Krishnamurti

I was born in 1948 to a Brahmin film-maker father and a Shia Muslim mother in free India just after the trauma of Partition. My parents were then living 'in sin' in the middle-class, Hindu locality of Mumbai's Shivaji Park, a place where religious and political leaders regularly made speeches about the greatness of India. My mother, fearing discrimination, cleverly concealed her identity behind a large bindi and mangalsutra, gave us all Hindu names, and sent me to an English-medium school run by Italian missionaries. I wasted eleven years of my life cramming for meaningless exams and learning meaningless values which did not operate either in my life, my teachers', the priests' or my parents'. They were trying to shape me into someone I was not and I grew up always feeling that I was not the person I longed to be. I was lonesome and spent all my energy trying to be less lonesome. This loneliness—and my hormones—hurled me into a teenage romance, an early marriage, parenthood and a disastrous start to my career in the film industry. I wanted to escape the pain and humiliation the reversals in my life inflicted on me and became part of the bogus, acid-dropping, enlightenment-seeking culture of the early 1970s. I experienced the mystical highs of LSD; I sought Osho, the sex guru, and the messiah of the no-messiah cult, Jiddu Krishnamurti. Unable to cope with the brutal truths that faced me, I dropped out of life even before the main credits had begun to roll.

One morning, as I was meditating, Pratap Karvat called. Pratap is a soft-spoken, meek man in a Woody Allen sort of way. I had met him by chance at a film shooting. I was reading the latest Jiddu Krishnamurti book, *The Awakening of Intelligence*, and Pratap wanted to take a look at it. We spoke about J.K., Rajneesh and then, perfectly ordinarily, he mentioned another Krishnamurti, U.G. Krishnamurti, who visited India every year but remained anonymous. Pratap asked over the telephone, 'U.G. is here, when would you like to meet him?' 'Now,' I replied. I used to be perennially unemployed and penniless and never had much to do.

I still remember my first meeting with U.G.; I can smell

the scent of tobacco, hear the clamour of the city and the squeaking of the stairs as I walked up the dark staircase. A volcanic silence roiled in my guts as I looked up the stairs and saw him standing at the top. In that silence my heart heard something. I have spent most of my life trying to understand what my heart heard that day. We went inside and settled down to listen to what U.G. had to say:

> I am not a godman; I would rather be called a fraud. The quest for god has become an obsessive factor in the lives of human beings because of the impossibility of achieving pleasure without pain. The messy thing called the mind has created many destructive things but the most destructive thing, by far, is god. God has become the ultimate pleasure. The variations of god, self-realization, moksha, liberation, the fashionable gimmicks of transformation, the first and the last freedom and all the freedoms that come in between, are pushing man into a state of manic depression. At some point in the course of evolution, man experienced self-consciousness for the first time—in contradistinction to the way consciousness is functioning in other species. It was there, in that division of consciousness, that god, along with the nuclear doctrine that is threatening the extinction of all that nature has created with such tremendous care, was born. Man is merely a biological being; there is no spiritual side to his nature. All your virtues, principles, beliefs, ideas and the spiritual values imposed on you by your culture are mere

affectations. They haven't touched anything in you. Religion exploited for centuries the devoutness, piousness and whole-souled fervour of the religious man. The future of mankind lies not in 'love thy neighbour as thyself' but in the terror that if you try to kill your neighbour, you will also be destroyed along with him. How long, is anyone's guess. No power on this earth, no god, no avatar, can halt this. Man is doomed.

That evening, for the first time since my acquaintance with Rajneesh, I found myself incapable of meditating. I kept hearing U.G. say, 'Meditation is warfare.' I wandered out into the streets. Later, I tried to sleep but couldn't. I knew my days with Rajneesh were numbered. My Bhagwan was dying within me and there was nothing I could do. Then, one day, I destroyed the mala given to me by Rajneesh and flushed it down the toilet. I was tired of the life I had been leading and of the man I had become. The years I had spent in Rajneesh's ashram had not contributed in any way towards my self-improvement. A chapter in my life had come to an end.

The news of my transgression reached the ashram and Rajneesh. Vinod Khanna, the actor, said with genuine concern, 'Why did you do that, Mahesh? I have never seen Bhagwan in such a temper. He wants you to come to the ashram and hand the mala back to him in person. He says he works so hard on you. If you don't retrieve and hand back the mala, he says he will destroy you.'

Rajneesh used to give discourses on unconditional love and had spoken at great length against being possessive. He was now behaving like a jilted lover. All along, he had just been peddling half-truths, high-sounding phrases and empty concepts. At this time U.G.'s words came to my rescue: 'A guru is one who tells you to throw away all crutches. He would ask you to walk and if you fall, he would say that you will rise and walk.' These words put me back on my feet.

Between 1977 and 1979 I met U.G. whenever he passed through Bombay. At that time I was still a struggling film-maker and made advertisement films to make ends meet. I was married and had a lovely daughter but I was having an affair with Parveen Babi, then a famous actor. Therefore, my personal life was a big mess, to put it mildly.

Rajneesh always insisted that love is unconditional. But when a film star made a pass at Parveen, I was angry enough to want to kill the man—and strangle Parveen. I lost my battle with jealousy and it became clear to me that my guru's teachings weren't working in my life any more.

I asked U.G., 'Is it possible for me to have sex, pleasure, companionship; exchange ideas and opinions with my girlfriend and yet be free from jealousy?'

'When someone makes a pass at your girlfriend or when you suspect infidelity, jealousy, hate and the agony are natural. To want to kill the man and the woman is a natural, healthy reaction, too. There would be something wrong with you if you felt differently for any reason, religious or otherwise,' said U.G. 'Culture has turned you into a hypocrite. And if some ugly saint of the marketplace says that there is a way out, that you can have sex and the rest of it and yet be free from jealousy, he is taking you for a ride. If jealousy must go, so must sex!' All I got from U.G. was despair. Every time I went to him he put my mental processes to rout. I had come to a dead end with no way to combat jealousy and despair. Perhaps the only way out was an act of recklessness. At two o'clock in the morning, I, drunk, walked to U.G.'s house and rang the doorbell. I told him, 'Why did I ever meet you? I come to you for solutions and end up with despair; I want to kill you.'

U.G. replied, 'Why don't you go to sleep, Mahesh. There is a sofa and a blanket. If you want to kill me, you can do so in the morning when there are people around. Then you can make the exercise a ritual.'

Minutes later I bid him goodnight and kissing his hand said, 'U.G., I love you.'

After I began to spend time with U.G., I gradually began to realize that his sagacity was not informed by years of experience and learning. There was something indefinable about him, a spontaneity and a peculiar peace that quietly seeped into the people who came to see him.

Questions began to bother me. What was the source of this peace? How or by what means had U.G. stumbled into this 'state' of being? Had his life been a preparation for this?

❧

'This boy is born to an immeasurably high destiny,' was the prediction made by Uppaluri Gopala Krishnamurti's mother before she died, seven days after his birth on 9 July 1918 in Masulipatam, a small town in south India. His maternal grandfather, Tummalapalli Gopala Krishnamurti, a wealthy Brahmin lawyer, took his daughter's deathbed prediction seriously and, convinced that U.G. was a yogabhrashta, one who had come very close to enlightenment in his past life, gave up a lucrative career to devote all his time to bringing him up. T.G. Krishnamurti believed greatly in the Theosophical movement but also adhered strongly to Hindu Brahminism. U.G. thus grew up with both traditions.

One day, as T.G. Krishnamurti meditated, a child began to cry, interrupting his concentration. He came down and thrashed the child severely. U.G., who was helplessly watching the incident, felt that the business of meditation had become hollow. The lives of the very people who preached the credo seemed to him shallow and empty. They spoke marvellously but a fear ruled their lives and their teachings had no place in their daily routines. These dilemmas became a search that lasted till U.G. was forty-nine.

Between the ages of fourteen and twenty-one, U.G. undertook all kinds of spiritual exercises. He was determined to find the truth about moksha, the state all great teachers of mankind had spoken about endlessly. He kept looking for someone who was an embodiment of this realization. U.G. spent seven summers in the Himalayas with Sivananda Saraswati, a Hindu evangelist and a strict, self-righteous spiritual 'authority'. He studied classical yoga and did tapas, meditation, in the caves of Rishikesh denying himself even the simple joys of life. He experimented with his body, going without food or water for several days, pushing his body to the limits of its endurance. Once, he even tried to live on grass! At that time he experienced certain mystical states but they came and went and touched no deep spiritual core. One day, U.G. caught his master Sivananda devouring some hot pickles behind closed doors—something that was banned to U.G. and all the other disciples. It was clear that his master was merely a hypocrite. U.G. left. He was intensely aware of the fact that he had meditated and performed penance, had experienced mystical states, but was, at the end of the day, no different from other people. He found himself caught up in conflict and greed. He was constantly angry and sex remained a nagging problem. U.G. thus describes the time: 'By twenty-one I had arrived at a point where I felt strongly that all teachers—Buddha, Jesus, Sri Ramakrishna, everybody—had deluded themselves and everybody around them. Everybody said, don't get angry, but I was angry all the time. What these people were telling me to be was false and because it was false, it would falsify me. I didn't want to live a false life. There would be no more shlokas, no religion, no practices. I accepted the reality that I was a brute and a monster. I was full of desire. I was finished with the whole business.'

Swami Ramana Padananda, U.G.'s friend, suggested that he should visit Sri Ramana Maharshi, who was then considered to be an enlightened soul. U.G. felt that the solutions were themselves the problem and was unconvinced about meeting Maharshi. But Padananda persisted. So U.G. reluctantly, hesitantly and unwillingly went to meet the great sage of Arunachal. Bhagwan Sri Ramana Maharshi was reading comic strips when U.G. first saw him. U.G. was immediately sceptical about any help from Maharshi. He sat there for two hours, watching the Bhagwan cut vegetables and play with this, that or the other, and he wasn't at all surprised to find that all those stories about how a look from this man could change one were untrue.

U.G. asked, 'Is there anything at all that can be called enlightenment?'

'Yes, there is,' replied Ramana.

'Are there any levels to it?'

The Master replied, 'No, no levels are possible. It is all one thing—either you are there or you are not there at all.'

Finally, U.G. asked, 'This thing called enlightenment, can you give it to me?'

Sri Ramana did not answer. After a pause, U.G. repeated the question, 'I am asking you whether you can give me whatever you have?' Looking U.G. in the eye, Bhagwan replied, 'I can give it to you but can you take it?'

'What arrogance!' U.G. thought to himself. Nobody had ever said anything like that to him before. For seven years he had practised all kinds of sadhanas, modes of meditation. He had also gone through a 'masochistic' period of self-denial. U.G. was convinced that if there was any individual qualified to attain that state, it was him. But greater doubts assailed him: what was the 'state'? What was it that Maharshi had? After all, Maharshi wasn't different from U.G.; he was a human, born of man. How could he ever be sure that there actually was something like enlightenment? He realized that if he was to find out, he would have to do it on his own. U.G. never visited Sri Ramana again. And after he left Tiruvannamalai, his real search began.

In the 1940s, U.G. quit his BA honours programme at Madras University and, because he had nothing better to do, began to work in Charles Webster Leadbeater's personal library at the headquarters of the Theosophical Society. After working for three months there, he worked as press secretary for George Sidney Arundale, then president of the Theosophical Society. In his mid-twenties, U.G. realized that sex was still something about which he could arrive at no resolution. Most religious traditions taught one to either deny sex or suppress it. Traditionalists saw it as an obstacle on the path of moksha. U.G. did not believe in denial; he only wanted to see what would happen to the urge if he did not do anything about it. The study of holy books, meditation, and complete abstinence did not help him in any way. Even the so-called mystical experiences he had had in his earlier years failed to resolve the sexual urge in him. He then came to terms with sex and understood it as a fundamental urge of the body which could never be false. Thus, in 1943, he married a beautiful Brahmin girl. The very next day after his wedding he realized that he had made a mistake.

U.G.'s association with the Theosophical Society, too, was rocky. He was joint secretary of the Indian division but continued to be critical of the Society. He was made national lecturer for the Society because of his gift for oratory and travelled extensively in India and Europe giving lectures but never really had his heart in his work. In May 1953, he met Curuppumullage Jinarajadasa in London, under whom he was working at the Theosophical Society, and expressed his desire to resign. Jinarajadasa tried to dissuade him and told U.G. that he should continue till he got back from America. But life willed otherwise and Jinarajadasa passed away in America. U.G. continued his lecture tour for the Theosophical Society in Europe. And then, one day, during a public lecture in Brussels, the inevitable happened. As U.G. spoke, it struck him that he could not possibly spend the rest of his life spouting this  second-hand information which anyone who cared to read a book could gather. He quit the Society.

In the late 1940s, towards the end of U.G.'s association with the Theosophical Society, J.K. arrived in India to give his first talk after the Second World War. J.K., who came from the Theosophists, was looked upon by them as the Buddha of the twentieth century. U.G. had been following J.K.'s lectures between 1947 and 1953. But after 1953, U.G. interacted with J.K. on a personal level, holding long conversations with him on several occasions. During that time, J.K. also met U.G.'s wife and their children and took particular interest in the health of their eldest son Vasant who suffered from polio. In all his interactions with J.K., the same question always surfaced in U.G.'s mind: What lay behind all the abstractions that J.K. spouted? Was there anything at all? From the way J. Krishnamurti described things, U.G. felt he had, to use the analogy of a popular proverb, seen the sugar but had never tasted it. U.G. felt like a blind man in a dark room looking for a black cat which was not there. But J.K.

asserted that the cat was very much present. U.G. repeated his question time and again, in one form or another, at every meeting with J. Krishnamurti, but never received a direct or satisfactory answer. U.G. would often lose his temper with J.K., becoming harshly, scathingly critical but J.K. was always the perfect gentleman. Though the relationship between the two cannot be called that of a guru and disciple, there is no denying the fact that J. Krishnamurti and his teachings had a great impact on U.G.; even though he gradually and progressively rejected it all in the end. The break came in Bombay when U.G., for the last time, asked J.K. to 'come clean for once [and tell me if] there is anything behind those abstractions'.

J.K. forcefully replied, 'You have no way of knowing it, sir.'

'If I have no way of knowing it and you have no way of communicating it, what the hell have we been doing? I've wasted seven years of my life listening to you. I am leaving for New York tomorrow.'

J.K., in his gentlemanly fashion, said, 'Have a pleasant journey and a safe landing, sir!'

U.G. was in America for five years. He lived there for the duration because his son was receiving treatment for polio. J. Krishnamurti occasionally tried to contact U.G. during this phase since he wanted information about the medical treatment and the progress of U.G.'s son. That was an interesting time to be in America, both culturally and politically. However, for U.G., America was like a transit camp, a sort of preparatory ground where he stripped himself of everything before going adrift in Europe. The money that U.G. had taken with him to the US was just enough to meet his son's medical expenses. So to keep the home fires burning, he did something he was best at: he gave lectures. Unlike India where his lectures used to be free, in those days, he would be paid a hundred dollars per lecture. However, after giving some sixty lectures in one year, U.G. felt exhausted and depressed with the whole business. Despite an overwhelming demand and good money, U.G. refused, saying that he no longer had the will to work. The onus of earning money for the family fell on Kusuma, U.G.'s wife. Kusuma, who had a degree in both English and Sanskrit, found a job with the World Book Encyclopedia. She was pregnant with her fourth child; she had to look after her son, and had left behind two daughters with a relative in India. She wasn't thrilled about having to go out to make a living but didn't have a choice. She took time off at the time of delivery and then resumed work while U.G. began to babysit. After some time, the inevitable happened; Kusuma quit her job in frustration and decided to leave America. The thought of her two daughters, who lived with her elder sister in India, troubled her all the time. And, to make matters worse, her husband was no longer the man she had married seventeen years ago. He had changed and was no better than a stranger, even in his own house. In 1959, Kusuma left the US, having failed to convince U.G. to come with her. U.G. bought her two tickets and gave her all the money he had with him. After his wife left, U.G. was offered a job with the World University. He had been recognized in the US as not only a great speaker but also one with a brilliant and well-informed mind. Since he wanted to now stay on in America he had no choice but to accept the offer. He then came to Madras to 'wind up' his show in Adyar. In Madras he met Kusuma, who had brought all her children along hoping that U.G. would change his mind. This was not to be, and this was U.G.'s last meeting with her.

In 1961, U.G. was in London, alone and penniless. 'There was no will to do anything. I was like a leaf blown here, there and everywhere.' One day, a policeman threw him out of Hyde Park. He had, at that time, just five pence in his pocket. The only place he could think of going to was the Ramakrishna Mission; he reached there at ten o'clock in the night. When he asked to see the Swami, the members of the Mission told him that he could not at that time in the night. However, as luck would have it, the Swami himself emerged. U.G. placed his scrapbook of newspaper cuttings on his background and lectures before the Swami. 'This was me, and this is me now.' 'What do you want?' the Swami asked U.G. He replied that he only wanted his permission to enter the meditation room for the night. The Swami explained that this was against the Mission's policy. However, he gave U.G. some money and offered him a room for the next day.

U.G. returned to the ashram at noon the next day and was invited for lunch. 'For the first time in a long time I had a real meal. I had lost even the appetite for food. It was almost as if I didn't know what hunger was or thirst was,' The Swami said that he was looking for a man with a background in Indian philosophy to help him bring out the Vivekananda centenary issue. While working on the centenary issue, U.G. was paid five pounds like the other swamis in the Mission. U.G. often used to wonder at the silliness of those meditating at the ashram. He himself was through with all this. Then, one day, he had a very strange experience in the meditation room. In his own words:

> I was sitting there doing nothing, looking at all those people, pitying them. I thought, these people are meditating. Why do they want to go in for samadhi? They are not going to get anything—I have been through all that—they are kidding themselves. I was sitting there and in my mind there was nothing, only blankness, when I felt something very strange: there was some kind of movement inside of my body. Some energy was coming up from the

> penis and out through the head, as if there was a hole on top of it. It was moving in circles in a clockwise direction and then in a counter-clockwise direction. It was such a funny thing for me. But I didn't relate it to anything at all. I was a finished man. Somebody was feeding me, somebody was taking care of me, there was no thought of the morrow. Yet, inside of me, something was happening.

After three months, U.G. said to the Swami, 'I am going. I can't do this kind of thing.' When U.G. left the Ramakrishna Mission in London, the Swami gave him fifty pounds.

The news of U.G.'s wanderings had reached Jiddu Krishnamurti through a common friend. Though U.G. had walked out on him, J.K. continued to keep tabs on U.G. and his family. However, U.G. was not particularly anxious to meet him. The next day Krishnamurti phoned him saying, 'You may come over. We shall go for a walk in Richmond Park and talk things over.' When U.G. went there that evening, it began raining heavily. Instead of going for a walk, they sat near the fireplace and talked. All of a sudden Krishnamurti asked, 'Why are you trying to detach yourself from your family?' U.G. looked at him. Evidently J.K. had no understanding of what was happening deep within him. 'I am not trying to detach myself. You can't understand me,' he said. 'Shall we go into the subject of why you are not attached to your family, sir?' Krishnamurti persisted. That was too much for U.G. 'Sorry,' he said, 'I haven't come here to discuss my family affairs with you. I am not here to seek any help from you.' That was U.G.'s last visit with Krishnamurti.

The following is the letter which U.G. wrote on 30 December 1961 to his wife, ending their relationship:

> I have received today on my return here your letter of 11 September 1961. It's quite obvious that I have failed to open your eyes and make you understand the reality of the situation. It hurts me to hear, from time to time, the suicide attempts of yours. But my detachment from you and my passive acceptance of your actions is a solid piece of fact. It is not apathy. There isn't a whiff of apathy in me. The bond of the family relationships has simply fallen away from me.
>
> I have thought long and hard about this matter. You know I am not the sort of person to be persuaded in these matters and I do not act on impulse. Let the marriage wither on the vine. Neither of us can bear to see the ravages of pain in the other. Let us prefer to cling to the memory of the past . . . I know you love me deeply. And I loved you dearly too in spite of our many bickerings and constant battles. But this 'broken wing fixation' will destroy you. You can't base your life on sentiment alone and that cannot be the basis of any marriage.
>
> We have known each other for eighteen years. It is impossible to forget the ties of those eighteen years. Old habits and memories have a strange way of surviving. I can never forget you, and I know nothing else will ever

equal my feelings for you in intensity. When we first met I liked you very much. That impression will continue, unchanged by anything that has happened since then.

Why is it, with all the will in the world, I cannot understand what is so obvious to you? Well, anyway, I would rather let things go to the devil in their own way than try to go back to the past. Since we get exactly what we ask for, no more and no less, there is no question of any atonement on my part for the way things have turned out. Everyone weaves his own destiny. If our children take beatings at the cruel hand of fate, I feel that I am not wholly responsible. They are as much your children as they are mine. Let not the idea that I have left you destitute overwhelm you. You have your own name, your degrees and your own properties. Why I acted the way I did and still act is difficult to grasp. But if they are held up against the mirror of my own peculiar interpretation, my actions show logic of their own. For all I know, life may not run on logic. Whether it is right or wrong, it in no way changes the pain of the situation. But there is nothing that I can do to change the course of events.

One more thought. Postponing a problem of course does not solve it. There is a way out of an unhappy marriage. When one partner breaks the law of commitment, the right accrues to the other of breaking the bond. The woman is not the husband's bond slave but his companion, and as an equal partner is as free as the husband to choose her own way of life. Since the new

> Hindu Code Bill provides for divorce, why don't you find some grounds either for divorce or legal separation? That would save a lot of mental anguish for us both. Do not for a moment think that I am asking you to do anything I would not do myself. But, personally, it does not matter to me one way or the other. There is no reason for me to return to India. Be happy and stay happy. I wish you the best and the finest.
>
> U.G.

U.G. never heard from Kusuma again. She died in 1963. No one knew where U.G. was at that time. One of his cousins who lived in England sent a letter addressed to a friend of U.G.'s in London informing him of his wife's death. His friend did not know of U.G.'s whereabouts. Six months later, when U.G. happened to visit him, his friend handed him the letter. The friend asked, 'What does the letter say?' U.G. replied, 'It says my wife died six months ago.' He wrote a letter to his children expressing his sympathy for their loss. His younger daughter wrote back telling him that Kusuma had gone into a state of deep despondency and depression and had to be hospitalized. She received electric shock treatments. She came out of the hospital within a few weeks of the treatment and died in an accident in which she broke her neck.

Whenever U.G. found himself slipping into old patterns of life, he quit and immediately moved on. He lived for a brief period in Paris and then in Geneva. There, he ran out of money and went to the Indian consulate. In the consulate he met Valentine de Kerven who was a translator there. She and U.G. soon became close friends. Valentine created a home for U.G. in Switzerland. She took care of U.G. but had no idea what was in the offing.

Madame Valentine de Kerven was a remarkable woman in her own right. Born in Switzerland in 1901, she was the daughter of a famous brain surgeon. Valentine left Switzerland for Paris at the age of eighteen to lead an independent life. She belonged to a group of artists and writers. She was interested in photography and modern art and was an active member of a French experimental theatre group. Valentine lived openly with a male friend which in those days was considered a social offence. She and her friend were the first to cross the uncharted Sahara desert on motorcycles. She made a documentary on gypsies and became the first female film producer in France. She also made documentary films on her father's medical research. She made an unsuccessful attempt to join the fight against Franco and the Fascists in Spain. In the 1950s, she drove from Switzerland to India, a trip which turned out to be the first of many she would make. U.G. Krishnamurti and Valentine de Kerven remained 'travelling companions with no destination' till the sunset of her life.

In 1953 U.G. was travelling through the beautiful valley of Saanen in the Alps when something in him said, 'Get off the train and spend some time here.' He did exactly that. While he was there he said to himself, 'This is the place where I must spend the rest of my life.' He had plenty of money then but his wife did not share his inclination. She hated the climate. Ever since, living in Saanen had remained an unfulfilled dream for U.G. And now, just like that, it had materialized. Valentine set up a house for U.G. in Saanen. One day, J. Krishnamurti arrived there. He began to hold talks and meetings in the Saanen valley every summer. U.G. at that time was not interested in Krishnamurti, or, for that matter, in anything. He was looking for nothing, and there was no desire to seek anything, yet he felt that something strange was happening to him.

During that time—he refers to it as the 'incubation period'—all kinds of things were happening within him—he had constant headaches and terrible 'pains in the brain'. He consumed huge quantities of aspirin to relieve himself, with no success. One day Valentine said to him, 'Do you know the amount of money you are spending on your aspirin and coffee? You are drinking fifteen cups of coffee every day. Do you know what it means in terms of money? It is three or four hundred francs per month. What is this?' U.G. could not explain to anybody the nature of the headaches he suffered in those days. He says, 'All kinds of strange things happened to me. I remember when I rubbed my body like this, there was a sparkle, like a phosphorous glow. Every time I rolled in my bed there was a spark of light. It was so funny. It was electricity—that is why I say it is an electromagnetic field. At first I thought it was because of my nylon clothes and static electricity; but then I stopped wearing nylon. I was a very sceptical heretic, to the tips of my toes. I never believed in anything. Even if I saw some miracle happen before me, I didn't accept that at all. It never occurred to me that anything of that sort was in the making for me.' Since the whole 'spiritual business' was out of his system, U.G. did not relate whatever was happening to him to liberation or moksha. But somehow, in spite of everything, at the back of his mind, the question about moksha or enlightenment persisted.

In April 1967, U.G. happened to be in Paris with Valentine. Some of his friends suggested that he should visit his old friend, J. Krishnamurti, who was there giving talks. As Valentine had never heard Krishnamurti before, U.G. thought that they should go. When they got there, they had to pay a two-franc admission charge to go in. U.G. was not ready for that. He said, 'Let's do something foolish. Let's go to Casino de Paris.' Even though it cost twenty francs, they went there. While watching the show U.G. had a strange experience: 'I didn't know whether the dancer was dancing on the stage or I was doing the dancing. There was a peculiar kind of movement inside of me. There was no division. There was nobody who was looking at the dancer.' This experience, which lasted till they came out of the theatre, puzzled U.G. The last time he had a dream was a week after this incident. In the dream he was bitten by a cobra and died instantly. His body was carried on a bamboo stretcher to the cremation ground. It was placed on a funeral pyre. The flame from the fire awakened him with a start. He found that his electric blanket was on high. This dream was a prelude to his 'death'.

In July, U.G.'s life went through another phase. The question, 'What is that state called moksha or enlightenment?' always had tremendous intensity for U.G. but it had no emotional overtones. The more he tried to find an answer, and the more he failed to find one, the more intense the question became. That year, J. Krishnamurti was again in Saanen, giving a series of lectures. One day U.G.'s friends dragged him to one. When U.G. listened to him he had this peculiar feeling that Krishnamurti was describing U.G.'s state and not his own. U.G. asked himself, 'Why did I want to know his state?' J.K. was describing 'movements', 'awareness', 'silence'. He said, 'In that silence there is no mind; there is action.' But U.G. said to himself, 'I am in that state. What the hell have I been doing these thirty or forty years, listening to all these people and struggling, wanting to understand his state or the state of someone else, Buddha or Jesus? I am in that state. Now I am in that state.' U.G. walked out of the tent. On his forty-ninth birthday, the day after he walked out of J. Krishnamurti's tent, U.G. was sitting on a bench under a tree overlooking the seven hills and seven valleys of Saanenland. In his own words:

> I was sitting there, and the whole of my being was the question: 'How do I know that I am in that state?' I said to myself, there is some kind of peculiar division inside of me: there is somebody who knows that he is in that state. The knowledge of that state—what I have read, what I have experienced, what they have talked about—it is this knowledge that is looking at that state, so it is only this knowledge that has projected that state. I said to myself, look here, old chap, after forty years you have not moved one step; you are still on square one. It is the same knowledge that projected your mind there when you asked this question. You are in the same situation, asking the same question, 'How do I know?' because it is this knowledge, the description of the state by those people which has created this state for you. You are kidding yourself. You are a damned fool. But there still was the peculiar feeling that this was the state.

U.G. didn't have any answer to the second question, 'How do I know that this is the state?' It was like a question in a whirlpool. It swirled numerous times and suddenly, the question disappeared.

According to U.G., 'The question disappeared. The

whole thing was finished for me and that was all. From then on, never did I say to myself, now I have the answer to all those questions.' The disappearance of his fundamental question, on discovering that it had no answer, was a physiological phenomenon, U.G. says: 'It was a sudden "explosion" inside, blasting, as it were, every cell, every nerve and every gland in my body.' And with that explosion, the illusion that there is continuity of thought, that there is a centre, an "I" linking up thoughts, was not there any more.' U.G. further says of this state:

> Then thought cannot link up. The linking gets broken and once it is broken, it is finished. Then it is not once that thought explodes; every time a thought arises, it explodes. So, this continuity comes to an end and thought falls into its natural rhythm.
>
> Since then I have no questions of any kind because the questions cannot stay there any more. The only questions I have are very simple questions like 'How do I go to Hyderabad?', questions necessary to function in this world. And people have answers for these questions. But for those ['spiritual' or 'metaphysical'] questions, nobody has any answers. So there are no questions any more.
>
> That is why I say that when this 'explosion' takes place (I use the word 'explosion' because it is like a nuclear explosion), it leaves behind chain reactions like a nuclear explosion. It shatters the whole body. It's not an easy thing; it's the end of man. Such a shattering blasts

every cell, every nerve in your body. I went through terrible physical torture at that moment. Not that you experience the 'explosion'; you can't experience the 'explosion' but only its after-effects. The 'fallout' changes the whole chemistry of your body.

I can say that because unless that wholesale change in the chemistry takes place, there is no way of freeing this organism from thought, from the continuity of thought. And since there is no continuity of thought, you can very easily say that something has happened but what actually did happen, I have no way of experiencing at all.

I really don't know what has happened to me. What I am telling you about is the way I am functioning. There seems to be some difference between the way you are functioning and the way I am functioning but basically there can't be any difference. How can there be any difference between you and me? But from the way we are trying to express ourselves, there seems to be some difference. I have a feeling that there is some difference, and what that difference is, is all that I am trying to understand.

U.G. noticed, during the week following the 'explosion', some fundamental changes in the functioning of his senses. On the last day his body went through a process of 'physical death' and the changes became permanent features.

For seven days, every day, a change occurred. U.G. discovered that his skin had become extremely soft, the blinking of the eyes had stopped and his senses of taste, smell and hearing had changed.

On the first day he noticed that his skin was so soft that it felt like silk and also had a peculiar kind of golden glow. 'I was shaving and each time I tried to shave, the razor slipped. I changed blades but it was no use. I touched my face. My sense of touch was different.' U.G. did not attach any significance to all this. He merely observed.

On the second day he became aware for the first time that his mind was in what he calls a 'declutched state'. He was upstairs in the kitchen, and Valentine had prepared some tomato soup. He looked at it and didn't know what it was. She told him it was tomato soup. He tasted it and then he recognized it. He swallowed the soup and he was back to that odd frame of mind. Rather, it was a frame of 'no mind'. He asked Valentine again, 'What is that?' She again said it was tomato soup. He swallowed again and forgot what it was. 'I played with this for some time. It was such a funny business—this "declutched state".'

That state became normal for U.G. He no longer spent time in reverie, worry, conceptualization and all the other kinds of thought processes people indulge in when alone. His mind would only engage when needed, as, for instance, when someone asked a question or when he had to fix something. When not needed, there was no mind, no thought—only life. On the third day, some friends of U.G. invited themselves over for dinner. He agreed to cook for them. 'But somehow I couldn't smell or taste properly. I became gradually aware that these two senses had been transformed. Every time some odour entered my nostrils, it irritated my olfactory centre in just about the same way. Whether the stimulus came from some expensive scent or from cow dung, it was the same irritation. And then, every time I tasted something, I tasted only the dominant ingredient—the taste of the other ingredients came later. From that moment on perfume made no sense to me and spicy food had no appeal for me. I could taste only the dominant spice, chillies or whatever it was. On the fourth day, something happened to his eyes. U.G. and his friends were sitting in the Rialto restaurant in Gstaad. It was here that U.G. became aware of a tremendous sort of 'vista vision', like a concave mirror.

> Things coming towards me, were moving into me, as it were. And things going away from me seemed to move out from inside of me. It was such a puzzle to me—as if my eyes were a gigantic camera, changing focus without my doing anything. Now I am used to the puzzle. Nowadays that is how I see. When you drive me around in your car, I am like a cameraman dollying along. The cars in the other direction go into me, and the cars that pass us come out of me. When my eyes fix on something they do it with total attention, like a camera.

That day, when U.G. came back home from the restaurant, he looked in the mirror to find that there was something odd about his eyes—they were 'fixed'. He kept looking in the mirror for a long time and observed that his eyelids were not blinking. He stared into the mirror and his eyes would still not blink for almost forty-five minutes. On the fifth day, U.G. noticed a change in his hearing. When he heard the barking of a dog, the barking seemed to originate inside of him. All sounds seemed to come from within him and nothing from outside.

The five senses changed in five days. On the sixth day U.G. was lying on a sofa. Valentine was in the kitchen.

> And suddenly my body disappeared. There was no body there. I looked at my hand. I looked at it—'Is this my hand?' There was no actual question but the whole situation was something like that. So I touched my body: nothing. I didn't feel there was anything there except the touch, the point of contact. Then I called Valentine and asked, 'Do you see my body on this sofa? Nothing inside of me says that this is my body.' She touched it and said, 'This is your body.' And yet that assurance didn't give me any comfort or satisfaction. I said to myself, 'What is this funny business? My body is missing.' My body had gone away, and it has never come back.

From then on, as far as his body was concerned, the points of contact were all that U.G. had, nothing else, because the sense of vision, he said, is independent of the sense of touch. So it was not possible for him to create a complete image of his own body because, in the absence of the sensation of touch, the corresponding points in his consciousness were missing.

And finally, on the seventh day, U.G. was again lying on the same sofa, relaxing, enjoying the 'declutched state'. Valentine would come in and he would recognize her as Valentine. She would go out of the room. When she made her exit, there was a blank, no Valentine. He would think, 'What is this? I can't even imagine what Valentine looks like.' He would listen to the sounds coming from the kitchen and ask himself, 'What are those sounds coming from inside me?' But he could not relate to them. He had discovered that all his senses were without a coordinating mechanism inside of himself; the coordinator was missing. And then, U.G. says:

> I felt something happening inside of me: the life energy drawing to a focal point from different parts of my body. I said to myself, 'Now you have come to the end of your life. You are going to die.' Then I called Valentine and said, 'I am going to die, Valentine, and you will have to do something with this body. Hand it over to the doctors; maybe they will use it. I don't believe in burning or burial. In your own interest you have to dispose of this body. One day it will stink. So, why not give it away?' Valentine replied, 'U.G., you are a foreigner. The Swiss government won't take your body. Forget about it.'

The frightening movement of his life force had come to a focal point. Valentine's bed was empty. He moved over to that bed and stretched out, getting ready to die. Valentine, of course, ignored what was going on. She left. But before she left, she said, 'One day you say this thing has changed, another day you say that thing has changed, and a third day you say something else has changed. What is all this? And now you say you are going to die. You are not going to die. You are all right, hale and hearty.' U.G. continues his account:

> Then a point arrived where it looked as if the aperture of a camera was trying to close itself. It is the only simile that I can think of. The way I am describing this is quite different from the way things actually happened at that time because there was nobody there thinking in such terms. All this, however, must have been part of my experience, otherwise I wouldn't be able to talk about it. So, the aperture was trying to close itself and something was there trying to keep it open. Then after a while there was no will to do anything, not even to prevent the aperture closing itself. Suddenly, as it were, it closed. I don't know what happened after that.

This process lasted for forty-nine minutes—this process of dying. It was like a physical death. U.G. maintained that it continued to happen to him even after that.

> My hands and feet became so cold, the body became stiff, the heartbeat slowed down, the breathing slowed down and then there was a gasping for breath. Up to a point you

> are there, you breathe your last breath, as it were, and then you are finished. What happens after that, nobody knows.

When U.G. came out of this, his landlady said that there was a telephone call for him. He went downstairs in a daze. He had been through a physical death and what brought him back to life, he didn't know. How long it lasted, he didn't know. 'I can't say anything about that because the experiencer was finished: there was nobody to experience that death at all'

U.G. used to refer to the events that happened to him during the summer of 1967 as the 'calamity':

> I call it 'calamity' because from the point of view of one who thinks this is something fantastic, blissful and full of beatitude, love or ecstasy, this is physical torture; this is a calamity from that point of view. Not a calamity to me but a calamity to those who have an image that something marvellous is going to happen. I can never tell myself or anybody that I'm an enlightened man, a liberated man, or a free man, or that I am going to liberate mankind.

On the eighth day he was sitting on the sofa and suddenly:

> There was a tremendous outburst of energy shaking the whole body and along with the body, the sofa, the chalet and the whole universse. You cannot cause that movement. Whether it was coming from outside or inside, from below or above, I didn't know, I couldn't locate the spot.

> It lasted for hours and hours. There was nothing I could do to stop it; I was totally helpless. This went on for days.

Then for three days U.G. lay in bed, his body contorted with pain. It was, he says, as if he felt pain in every cell of his body. Similar outbursts of energy occurred intermittently throughout the next six months whenever he lay down or relaxed. U.G. explained that thought had controlled his body to such an extent that when that control loosened, all of his metabolism went awry. Then the movement of his hands changed. They started turning backwards. 'That is why they say my movements are mudras.' Certain hormonal changes started occurring in his body. Now he didn't know whether he was a man or a woman. Suddenly there was a breast growing on the left side of his chest. It took three years for his body to finally fall into a new rhythm of its own. His friends observed swellings up and down his torso, neck and head, at those points called chakras. These swellings of various shapes and colours came and went at regular intervals. On his lower abdomen, the swellings were horizontal, cigar-shaped bands. Above the navel was a hard, almond-shaped swelling. A hard, blue swelling, like a large medallion, in the middle of his chest was surmounted by another smaller, brownish-red, medallion-shaped swelling at the base of his throat. These two 'medallions' were as though suspended from a varicoloured, swollen ring—

blue, brownish and light yellow—around his neck, like in the pictures of some Hindu gods, There were other similarities: his throat was swollen to a shape that made his chin seem to rest on the head of a cobra, as in the traditional images of Shiva. Just above the bridge of the nose was a white lotus-shaped swelling. All over the head the small blood vessels expanded, forming patterns like the stylized lumps on the heads of some statues of the Buddha. Like the horns of Moses and the Taoist mystics, two large and hard swellings periodically appeared and disappeared. The arteries in his neck, blue and snake-like, expanded and rose into his head. U.G. said that his body was affected by everything that was happening around it: 'Whatever is happening there is also happening here—there is only the physical response. This is affection. You can't prevent this, for the simple reason that the armour that you have built around yourself is destroyed; so it is very vulnerable to everything that is happening.'

In his discussions with medical doctors U.G. learned that the ductless glands are located in exactly the same spots where the Hindus speculated that the chakras are. The thymus gland, it is said, is very active when one is a child. Therefore, children have extraordinary feelings. When they reach puberty, the gland becomes dormant—at least that's what scientists say. When this sort of explosion takes place within the body, which the scriptures refer to as being born again, that gland is automatically activated so that all the extraordinary feelings come back. 'Feelings are not thoughts, not emotions; you feel for somebody. If somebody hurts himself there, that hurt is felt here—not as a pain but there is a feeling. You automatically say, "Ouch!"'

There is an incident in U.G.'s life which illustrates this. He was once staying at a coffee plantation in south India. For some reason a mother started beating her child. She was angry and she hit her child so hard that the child almost turned blue. Somebody then asked U.G., 'Why did you not interfere and stop her?' U.G. answered, 'I was standing there, puzzled: whom should I pity, the mother or the child?' Both were in an awkward situation; the mother could not control her anger and the child was so helpless. Then I found all marks corresponding to the marks of the beatings on my back. So I too was a victim of that beating.' For U.G., this was possible because consciousness cannot be divided. 'With this affection, there is no question of your sitting in judgement on anyone.'

U.G. often said that the 'third eye', also called the ajna chakra, is the pituitary gland. When once the interference of thought is gone, the function of thought is taken over by this gland: it is this gland, and not thought, that gives the instructions or orders to the body. That is why they call it ajna, command, chakra. According to U.G., there is the built-in armour created by thought which prevents us from being affected by things: 'Since there is nobody here who uses thought as a self-protective mechanism, thought burns itself up. It undergoes combustion, ionization. Thought is, after all, a vibration. So when this ionization of thought takes place it throws out, and sometimes covers the whole body with, an ash-like substance. There is tremendous heat in the body as a result of this.' One of the major reasons why U.G. spoke of this 'calamity' in pure and simple physical and physiological terms is that it had no psychological or religious overtones. Such a thing, U.G. said, must have happened to many people. It was not something that one could especially be prepared for. There was no sadhna necessary for such a thing to happen.

For U.G., the most puzzling and bewildering part of the 'calamity' was when the sensory activities began functioning independently. There was no coordinator linking up the senses. That presented a problem to Valentine. 'We'd go for a walk and I'd look at a flower and ask her, "What's that?" She'd say, "That's a flower." I'd take a few more steps, look at a cow and ask, "What's that?" Like a baby, I had to relearn everything.' Valentine didn't understand what was going on. She consulted a leading psychiatrist in Geneva. The psychiatrist told her that unless he saw the person he couldn't be of help; he asked her to bring U.G. over. But U.G. declined because he knew that something extraordinary had happened inside him. His difficulty was that the people who came to see him didn't seem to understand the way he was functioning and he didn't seem to understand the way they operated. Summing up his 'calamity', U.G. said:

> And that's all there is to it. My biography is over. There is nothing more to write about and there never will be. If people come and ask me questions, I answer. If they don't, it makes no difference to me. I have no particular message for mankind except to say that all holy systems for obtaining enlightenment are nonsense and that all talk of arriving at a psychological mutation through awareness is rubbish. Psychological mutation is impossible. The natural state can happen only through biological mutation.

The incredible physiological changes continued to occur for years. U.G. was so bewildered by what had happened to him that he did not speak for a year after the 'calamity'. He had to practically learn to think and talk all over again, so complete was the change. After a year or so, he had regained most of his communicative powers. Yet he did not say much. 'What remains to be said after an experience like this?' he asked. One day the answer came in a flash: 'I'll say it exactly the way it is.' Except for a year's break in the late 1960s, U.G. spoke tirelessly ever since. Of all this U.G. said later:

> I did not know what was happening to me. I had no reference point at all. Somehow I died and came back to life, free of my past. This thing happened without my

> volition and despite my religious background. And that is a miracle. It cannot be used as a model and duplicated by others.

So, after his quest of forty-nine years and his extraordinary physiological transformation, what did U.G. have to offer to the world which is desperately looking for something to keep it from falling apart? U.G., when asked about what had happened to him as a result of the 'calamity', usually took recourse to the 'Peanuts' cartoon and said: 'I don't know why it happened or when it happened or how it happened. I don't even know what happened. Did something happen?' U.G. often took recourse to this Indian parable to illustrate his point:

> Once, twelve children were playing in an uninhabited part of a village. There they discovered an image of Ganesh, the elephant god, the god of beginnings. They started dancing and singing around this image. The pot-belly of the god's image attracted the attention of one of the boys; out of curiosity he stuck his finger in the idol's navel. He felt something sting his finger. He instantly withdrew his finger from the navel. Instead of crying out in pain, he pretended to his playmates that something extraordinary had happened to him. The boy closest to him followed suit. One after another all the boys tried the same; except for the last—the youngest. 'It's a scorpion!' he cried. Everyone nodded their heads and they all began to cry.

U.G. is like the little boy who is screaming to the world that he has been 'stung by a scorpion'. Excerpts from the book, *Thought is Your Enemy*, replay that 'scream':

> Whatever has happened to me has happened *despite* everything I did. Whatever I did or did not do and whatever events people believed led me into this are totally irrelevant. It is very difficult for me to fix a point now and tell myself that this is me and look back and try to find out the cause for whatever happened to me. That is why I am emphasizing all the time that it is *acausal*. It is something like, to use my favourite phrase, lightning hitting you. But one thing I can say with certainty is that the very thing I searched for all my life was shattered to pieces. The goals that I had set for myself, self-realization, god-realization, transformation, radical or otherwise, were all false. And there was nothing there to be realized and nothing to be found there. The very demand to be free from anything, even from the physical needs of the body, just disappeared. And I was left with nothing. Therefore, whatever comes out of me now depends on what you draw out of me.
>
> I have actually and factually nothing to communicate, because there is no communication possible at any level. The only instrument we have is the intellect. We know in a way that this instrument has not helped us to understand anything. So when once it dawns on you that that is not the instrument and there is no other instrument to understand anything, you are left with this puzzling

situation that there is nothing to understand. In a way it would be highly presumptuous on my part to sit on a platform, accept invitations and try to tell people that I have something to say.

What I am left with is something extraordinary—extraordinary in the sense that it has been possible for me not through any effort, not through any volition of mine. Everything that every man thought, felt and experienced before has been thrown out of my system.

There is no teaching of mine and never shall be one. 'Teaching' is not the word for it. A teaching implies a method or a system, a technique or a new way of thinking to be applied in order to bring about a transformation in your way of life. What I am saying is outside the field of teachability. It is simply a description of the way I am functioning. It is just a description of the natural state of man. That is the way you, stripped of the machinations of thought, are also functioning.

Your natural state has no relationship whatsoever with the religious states of bliss, beatitude and ecstasy. They lie within the field of experience. Those who have led man on his search for religiousness throughout the centuries have perhaps experienced those religious states. So can you. They are thought-induced states of being and as they come, so do they go. The timeless can never be experienced, can never be grasped, contained, much less given expression to by any man. That beaten track will lead you nowhere. There is no oasis situated yonder. You are stuck with the mirage.

'Doesn't an encounter with you help people in any way in their quests?' I asked U.G. in Carmel, where I was spending forty days with him in the process of writing a book. He said, 'Look, during your stay here, you have learned to make coffee, toast your bread, use the washing machine and wash your dishes like anybody else. These are the only things you will learn from me. My way of life and what I am saying will not help people to face the difficult situations in their lives. If there is any potential in them, it will surface. But this doesn't apply to spiritual progress or potential because that doesn't exist. If you are a murderer, you will murder with finesse. This doesn't mean that I condone murder but whatever is there in you will bloom.' When I look back at those days of my life I know for certain that had it not been for U.G., I wouldn't be here today. I wouldn't have bloomed and become what I am. If today I have the audacity to live life on my own terms, without imposing my creed on anyone, it is because of the priceless insights I have assimilated through my fierce and passionate confrontations with him. He bailed me out from the quagmire that I was in when Parveen Babi was sinking into the abyss of madness and was dragging me into it with her. Like a parent he pulled me out and then amputated me from the relationship, earning a bad name for himself in the process, but pushed me back on to my shaky, bruised feet to start life all over again. I remember once, when I was on the brink of throwing in the towel and giving up, he said, 'I'll never forgive you if you don't become successful, Mahesh.' He said that with such love that from that day the sentence became my lodestar for all the dark nights that followed. When I became a somebody, he would show me off like a trophy and boast to those around him like a proud parent, saying, 'This guy was wasting his time with Rajneesh just hanging around and doing nothing and look where he is today. The only thing that an encounter with a man like me does is to help you to fit into that brutal world out there, where you will be able to deal with the realities on a day-to-day basis and cope with it, and not look for some utopian world which will make you into a misfit.' One day, we were walking on the streets of Hollywood when I told him of my dissatisfaction with my work and my life. The desire to make those inane movies was fast withering within me. He told me to leave whilst I was still on the top and make way for tomorrow. I did. I made *Zakhm,* an intensely personal film which locked horns with the right-wing forces which were ruling the country in those days, succeeded in dismantling its fierce opposition, and went on to win several National Awards. And then, while the hall was still echoing with applause, I quit. And that's why I'm still here, creating new talent and helping young people to find their own potential. 'Every prostitute has her time,' U.G. said. 'You have done well by pulling the lifeline out of your directorial career and dedicating yourself to scouting and nurturing fresh talent.'

For thirty years of my life, I woke up every day thinking of him and talking to him, keeping in touch with him wherever he went. He was the fulcrum that my entire world revolved around. But like every good parent or mentor he slowly started to wean himself away from me. He saw to it that my visits and my phone calls became less and less frequent. But in spite of that he always remained my lifeline whom I would reach out to when I needed the courage to take the world on. He patted me on my back for turning down the prayer breakfast meeting invitation from George W. Bush just before the Iraq war. But little did the world know that whatever courage I got, I got from him.

And then, on my fifty-seventh birthday, I called him. I had telephoned him after a very long time. Something within me compelled me to make this call. We were chatting and I said, 'U.G., you once told me that when I put fifty-six years behind me and turn fifty-seven, my destiny will take over. You also said that thereafter I will have no control over my life.' 'Yes, I did,' he said without a pause. It seemed as if he had been waiting for my call. 'From now on I have no role to play in your life. If you try and shape the events of your life and give it some kind of direction, you will have trouble. Let your life take over.'

'Do you mean to say that hereafter you have absolutely no role to play in my life?' I asked.

'None whatsoever. Good luck!' he said, and hung up.

His words had a sense of finality. They made me feel sad and exhilarated at the same time. I felt like a child who can now pedal away on his bicycle into the unknown without the support of his parents. A new phase in my life had commenced.

❧

U.G. Krishnamurti lived the last years before his death in March 2007 the way he lived his entire life: he travelled constantly, moving spontaneously from place to place, and ran his life on his own terms. He was only slightly slowed down by age—he was now eighty-eight. He would say from time to time, 'There is such a thing as old age!' But his movements belied his words. He perhaps would have wished to visit America one last time but air travel and navigating airports had become increasingly problematic for him. He did not want anyone even to carry his suitcase, let alone keep him from falling.

In 2004, in the Black Forest, U.G. lost his balance and fell the first time when he was alone in his room at night. He fell again in 2005 in Gstaad and endured a lengthy, painful, but good-natured recovery process, surrounded by friends he had summoned from all over the world, who wondered if the 'end' was near. 'Time for this old man to go,' he would say again and again, but his high energy and vitality said otherwise. He was soon on his feet again and travelling. But as his physical strength began to ebb and balance became uncertain, it became evident that his precious independence would be compromised.

In January 2007, U.G. visited Vallecrosia, Italy, on the Mediterranean coast close to the French border. He was staying in the apartment arranged for him by his friends Lucia and Giovanni in their family villa. On 31st of January, U.G. fell once again at 4 a.m. while washing his underwear in his bathroom. He was seriously injured but pulled himself to the doorway of his living room, unlocked the door, but was unable to stand up. An Israeli friend of his found him in this condition and helped him to the couch. Though his leg healed somewhat, he never regained his strength. When he realized his health was rapidly deteriorating he called his family and friends from all over the world to come and say goodbye to him. He refused any and all medical help and intervention. There were many doctor friends coming and going but he would take no advice from them or from astrologers or healers. He said, 'I never manipulated my body in my life and I will not manipulate it in my death.' U.G. always spoke about how he wanted to have none of the complications of civilization surrounding his passing on. And though he wanted very much to return to Gstaad to die, it became evident that he was becoming weaker and weaker and his journey would not be possible. He accepted this fact, as he always accepted the inevitable in any situation. He then began the process of orchestrating his own death.

A Taste of Life

10 February 2007, Mumbai

'Mahesh, U.G. called. He wants Suguna and I to come to Italy right away. He is sending us the air tickets. He says it is time to say the final goodbye. Will you talk to him and figure the situation out?' Chandrasekhar—whom I affectionately call Babu—says in a tremulous voice over the phone. He was shaken by the very idea of saying the 'last goodbye' to the most important relationship of his life. 'Give me the number where I can reach him,' I say, pulling myself out of my bed. Minutes later, as I begin to call Italy, I discover that I am unfazed. It could be because U.G. had promised me that he would not leave this planet without meeting me. He hadn't asked me, and I knew the end was not yet near. After incessant trying, my call to Italy finally comes came through. The manner in which Mario greets me over the phone confirms that things are just fine.

'U.G., it is Mahesh,' I hear him scream.

When he comes to the phone, I say, 'U.G., you cannot die without meeting me. You gave me your word that you would summon me when the end is close. You cannot say goodbye without having that "last scene" with me.'

He says, 'My body is giving me trouble; I want to get rid of it. I am better but I still cannot walk or move. I am not coming to India nor am I going to America. I will go back to Gstaad after two weeks.'

'Do you want me to come see you?' I ask.

'I will call you,' he says.

As he hands the phone back to Mario, I can hear him repeat what I have told him. There is laughter in his voice. As I hang up, I realize that because of this man, I have come a long way. There was a time when the very idea of his death would make me hit the bottle and I would drink till I passed out. Today I am dealing with that idea with unusual calm.

11 February 2007, Mumbai

I am spearheading Bollywood's war against those forces which strangle creative thought. For the first time in the history of Indian cinema, all the associations have come together on a common platform to lock horns with the right-wing forces in Gujarat. 'If *Parzania* is not released in Gujarat, no Hindi film will be screened there,' is my call. Many have come out in the open to back me on this. Just when I taste a kind of victory on this front, I get the news that U.G.'s health has deteriorated.

'Do you want me to come to Italy?' I ask him. The subtext is loud and clear: are you dying, old chap?

'Come along with Babu and Suguna to Italy,' he says.

My heart says that he is still far away from the final fade-out. I call Paul Lynn. Lynn is a medical doctor and used to be a 'seeker' once—U.G. helped him to restart his life. He is a millionaire now and the sanest amongst the group present there; he will tell me how bad things really are.

'I just got here two hours ago. He looks weak. I have never seen him this bad. I would not be surprised if he goes tomorrow. But there are chances that he may get out of this.'

'Tell him he can't die without having that last scene with me. If he does, the movie of my life will be a big flop,' I say. Lynn laughs.

Late that night I receive an SMS: 'Gave him your message. He said, "My god!" and went back to sleep.' I call Mukesh, my brother, who is shooting for our film *Awarapan* in Hong Kong and tell him that I will be leaving for Italy.

'The office will fix everything. Just go,' he says. He

understands what this news means to me. The night is still.

14 February 2007, Mumbai

We are not scheduled to land in Italy till the 23rd of February. I wake up in the morning to find Paul's mail in my inbox.

> Dear Mahesh,
>
> U.G. seems to have stabilized at the moment and is awaiting the crowds. At least fifteen are arriving tomorrow from all over and it's already a full house. It should be less by the time you get here. We need your realistic and blunt assessment of the situation.
>
> It looks as if U.G. will be here for another two weeks at least. By then he should know whether he can make the journey to Gstaad. I think he prefers to go there into his cave and not see so many people. Then he can find out whether he can rally once more.
>
> All the best,
>
> Paul

Later in the day I call Robert Carr, Bob, one of U.G.'s oldest friends. 'Let's meet and talk things over,' he says. Bob met U.G. in the summer of 1966 in the quaint village of Saanen in Switzerland after attending a talk by J. Krishnamurti. His life has never been the same since. I go to his pad in the suburbs of Mumbai that evening.

Both of us are deeply aware that we are in a very important phase of our lives. We begin to talk about U.G. and the impact the news of his possible death has had on us. Then, just like that, I begin to speak. I tell Bob that I have no desperate desire to go to U.G. and play out a scene where the master divulges his secrets to the weeping disciple, filling him and the generations to come with imperishable wisdom. Buddha left behind a weeping Ananda who, despite his proximity to Buddha, failed to understand the core message of Buddhism: Everything perishes; whatever is born must die. U.G., however, connected me to an inner strength. He made me stand on my own two feet. The light that I now have within me may have come from the insights I have acquired over the many days I spent with him but it is truly and only mine. To make U.G. a god and to turn his passing away into a glowing, sacred moment would nullify everything that he stood for and spoke about. 'There's nothing to this man called U.G.,' he once said to me under a wintry sky in Gstaad, 'when he dies he will rot in the field like any garden slug or field mouse. You cannot use what he has said to bring about change in yourself or in the world.' I say all this and more to Bob before driving back home.

In the evening U.G. calls to insist that I hurry things up and come to Italy as soon as possible. At midnight he calls again. 'Come now. Don't wait for the others.'

16 February 2007, Mumbai

Today is Mahashivratri, the day of Lord Shiva. Things in Italy are not looking too bright. Paul's letter to Bob reveals the ground reality.

Hi,

It's just going to be crazy here through to the end of the month. It might get better after the 26th or so. I think Mahesh is coming with Suguna and Babu and Bulbul on the 23rd or near then. It's impossible to predict what will happen in two weeks. I'm pretty sure U.G. will stay here till the end of the month. It will depend then whether he has the strength to travel to Gstaad, which he wants to do. In Gstaad I think he wants to have very few around him. Maybe you should think about Gstaad rather than here. If you fly to Milan you then have another three-hour car ride to come here and that also will cost you about $100 each way because of the gas and road toll cost. The hotel cost is not so bad for Europe, it would be about $40 a night, maybe less. Gstaad would be the same for hotel, if it's not high season. If you only come to Gstaad, you could fly into Zurich, Geneva or possibly Frankfurt, which gives you more airline choices. I guess its best to wait a while and see what happens. In the meantime check out if there are any cheaper flights to other places. U.G. is slightly better today but I'm not optimistic. It just seems like he is closing up shop, slowly.

All the best,

Paul

23 February 2007, Mumbai

Paul,

If the old man is alive and kicking and not threatening to go, why should one come to that horrible place? Just a question. Can you pitch it to him please?

Love,

Mahesh

I am working on my script for *Dhoka*. A message arrives. It is from Paul: 'The old man says you need not come; he can die first. Your question got him all worked up. The devoted types were shocked but I loved the burst of energy.' The SMS jolts my being. It is time for me to drop everything and leave.

Nine Days in Vallecrosia

27 February 2007, Vallecrosia, Italy

Dawn is breaking over Milan. As I step out of the aircraft, I realize that it is not as cold here as they said it would be. Much ado is made about the European winter. My connecting flight to Nice is at 10.10 a.m.—I have lots of time to kill. I while away my time in the Alitalia lounge. Mukesh has warned me to be careful of Italian thieves. He once lost all the money he had in this very lounge. I don't think I will be setting my eyes on the old man before 2.00 p.m. I wonder why he has summoned me. Bob says it is 'to close shop'.

As I wait to board my flight to Nice, three young men from Punjab who work in a restaurant in some small town in Italy approach me. They take pictures with me and express their pleasure at having seen me in person. The news of the Congress Party's dismal performance in the polls in Punjab has reached them here in Milan. I call Nadeem Javed, the bright, likeable president of the Congress-backed National Students' Union of India in New Delhi. He sounds depressed. 'I don't know about the Congress but you certainly have a bright future, Nadeem,' I tell him, trying to lift his sagging spirits. The plane that is going to carry us to Nice is a tiny one; in fact, it looks like a toy plane. From up here in the sky, Nice looks like a pretty city. Paul receives me on my arrival. As we drive through the outskirts of this famous French city and head towards Vallecrosia, Paul begins to give me the lowdown on U.G.'s condition for the past one month. What I gather from him is that U.G.'s health has been on a see-saw. Some days he is absolutely fine and then, suddenly, his health goes on a downward spiral. The look in Paul's eyes reveals much more than his words do.

The house U.G. is living in reminds me of the house featured in Francis Coppola's enduring cinematic masterpiece *The Godfather*. A lemon tree with much fruit stands outside U.G.'s 'cave' like a guard. It's lunchtime. Friends from all over the world have assembled here in this quiet town to say what some think of as their 'last goodbye' to U.G. Suddenly I'm face to face with him. He is lying sprawled on his big white couch, propped up by a big grey pillow. He has lost a lot of weight. The clothes he is wearing literally hang on him. There is much sunshine in the room. I suddenly feel the need to go to him and kiss his feet. As I do that, I notice that for the first time his body does not recoil.

'Thank god he doesn't have the energy to say no to me,' I say, trying to lighten the mood. 'You're not going to die! Why are you threatening to die and not dying?' I ask.

'It's not in my hands,' he responds, 'it's in yours.' He then promptly and very typically switches to a very mundane topic which he would like everyone to believe is more important than his deteriorating health. He chides me. He pulls me up for not using my name, power and fame to get his friends, Chandrasekhar, Suguna and his daughter Bulbul, Italian visas. I try to explain to him why I was unable to do so but he doesn't relent. He has always told me that fame and power, if not used to get things done, are no good. As silence descends, I look into his eyes and ask him, 'So, what is the secret, U.G.?' Unlike sages who, through the history of mankind, have given their devotees priceless wisdom in their parting moments, which with time became the bedrock on which lofty religious institutions and religious movements were built, my old man stares back at me and very simply says, 'There is no secret. I'm just waiting to say goodbye to you.' Unable to contain the overflowing affection I feel for him, I lovingly reach out and kiss his forehead. 'Aye!'

he says shyly, 'did you see what he did?' he asks the room full of people watching our exchange with great warmth and interest. Like a director who is not very happy with a shot, he asks for a 'retake' of my action. He then says something he has never said to anyone in his life before. He looks at me and then pointedly at everyone else and tells me, 'Fall at my feet again.' I obediently do as I am told. I reach for his foot as if it's my universe and cuddle it. The only difference I feel this time is that I feel his other foot affectionately tapping my head in the manner that a mother would lull her child to sleep.

'This is not how a dying man dies, U.G.,' I say, getting back on my feet.

'This is the way to die,' he says, looking into my eyes. The message is loud and clear.

Moments later, I sit at his feet as I have always done, listening to him. He seems frail but nowhere do I see any sign of his ferocity ebbing.

He asks me, 'Why do you want to imitate some other bastard?'

I reply, 'That's all we can do.'

'That's all that you have been made to believe and asked to do. All that shit that culture has put into your system is what defines you. The leaders of mankind and the caretakers of culture are the filthiest bastards. And it is they who are responsible for your tragedy. And all that junk and garbage cannot be flushed out of your system through any effort or volition of yours.'

I ask, 'So, is culture asking you only to be a perfect imitation of the models they have placed before you?'

He answers me with a question of his own: 'Have they succeeded in making you do that? Be honest, have they?'

'By pretending to be like them I fool myself and fool the world that they have. But if I were to be actually honest, they have not succeeded. I am nothing but a monkey of my own ideals.'

At this point he turns towards Larry Morris, an American who, apart from being a poet, also runs a church in Albuquerque, New Mexico, and says, 'Not one teeny-weeny bit of what he says from the pulpit in his church operates in his life. He is only repeating all that to make a living. And he should be thankful to Jesus since he has provided him with a means to earn an easy living.'

My attention is drawn to his legs. They look thin, with almost no muscle. He has hardly eaten for days. 'Which foot of yours is broken?' I ask, looking at his feet.

'Not broken,' he says in a ringing voice. I quickly correct myself. 'I'm sorry, which foot is hurt?' He points to his left leg. I am reminded of a picture of U.G. that was sent to me by friends before his fall. In the picture he was balancing a football on his left foot like a professional.

28 February 2007, Vallecrosia

It was a peaceful night that left no residue of fatigue in the body. The roar of the Mediterranean Sea punctuates the silence. Its blue expanse stretches into the horizon just outside my window. My body clock pushes me out of bed according to the Indian standard time. It is 5.00 a.m. here and 9.30 a.m. in Mumbai. Getting used to a new place is like getting to know a new person. Narayana Moorty, our friend who is a professor of philosophy in California and with whom I'm sharing this modest pad, shows me how to use the cooker and how to manipulate the dysfunctional shower in our bathtub.

A pink dawn is breaking over U.G.'s cottage which he calls his 'cave'. It is 6.45 a.m. and the room is already full of people. 'How was your night, U.G.?' I ask.

'I got up from my couch and sat down on the seat and shat,' he says.

'Wow, that is one hell of an achievement,' I say.

Then, just like that, Chandrasekhar, Babu, surfaces in our conversation. 'He's like Julie. He's holding on to all those audio and video tapes. He must get rid of them,' says U.G. I call Babu and warn him playfully not to risk coming to Italy, since the old man seems determined to make him part with all his treasures. 'But I don't have those tapes, Mahesh! I just have a copy of what I've given away,' he wails over the phone, petrified by what may be in store for him on his arrival in Vallecrosia.

'He wants people to let go of him,' says Laxmi, fixing me a cup of coffee. 'This is his way of making them do it.' Laxmi is Guha's charming wife. This Indian American couple, who have made a life for themselves in New Jersey, have been regulars in U.G.'s inner circle. U.G. is offering 300,000 dollars to anyone who kills him. He does not want to be dependent on people. U.G. says, with fierce emphasis, 'You guys serve people to feel good. You have been brainwashed to help the helpless. You experience the "do-gooders' high" every time you nurse or attend to the frail and the vulnerable.'

Paul Lynn, who has known U.G. since even before 'calamity', says, 'When we asked him what happened to him, he said that he found out that he, U.G., does not exist. He never did!' Unable to comprehend this bizarre, absurd statement, I turn to U.G. and ask, 'Are you serious when you say this?' The old man hits me on my head with lightning speed. Having done that, he asks mischievously, 'Tell me now, do I exist or do I not?' His gesture makes everyone laugh and leaves me dumbfounded. It is impossible to cope with his crazy wisdom.

The time for Laxmi and Guha to leave arrives. Laxmi senses that this may be the last goodbye. She does what her heart desires the most—she falls at U.G.'s feet and begins to cry. U.G. tries to lighten the mood by saying, looking at me, 'Hey, look at what she's doing! Ask her to stop.' I can see that he is affected by the genuineness of her gesture. I tell Laxmi not to hold back and to do exactly what she has been longing to for years. U.G.

yields and then almost gives her a recipe to live her life. 'Go,' he says, 'look after your children. They're such brilliant children.' Guha, ever-smiling, hangs hungrily on to U.G.'s every word. His eyes suddenly glisten with tears. U.G. then waves the couple away with a graceful gesture, gently nudging them back into the stream of their lives.

Most of the Westerners present who are not familiar with an overt display of the submerged side of human emotions are taken aback. It is also quite uncharacteristic of U.G. to allow such a show of emotion where he is concerned but I guess I have raised the bar by kissing his feet, not once but twice, on my arrival. That seems to have emboldened the people around him. But the truth is that U.G. has always been open to anything real. With him, there was no room for falsities.

'How is U.G., Papa?' asks Pooja on the phone. I can sense from her voice that she is genuinely concerned. She is perhaps the only one amongst my children who knows how much U.G. means to me. And amongst all my kids, she has spent the most time in U.G.'s presence. She still speaks about her first trip to the United States when she was eighteen, which U.G. made so memorable for her. She tasted cheesecake for the first time then and also swindled him out of a hundred dollars—which U.G. knew about but let pass! In a stand-off, U.G. always sided with her, advising her, 'Ignore your father. Just do what your heart says.' There is no denying that being exposed to U.G. in her formative years has emboldened Pooja and gone a long way in making her the fearless person that she is today. 'He's fine, Pooja. Don't worry, he won't die so soon. There is still much harassment he has to subject us to,' I say jokingly, with an element of hope too, I guess.

I'm seized with this overpowering urge to give U.G. comfort. I reach out and press his feet with my hand. 'First it hurts and then it feels good,' U.G. says. And then, he suddenly does what he has never done: he pushes the other foot towards me and says, 'Now, press this one!' Everyone is struck by this and so am I.

As the evening deepens, voices whisper that he's getting better. But somehow this new-found optimism fails to erase the dread that is welling up within me. Later, my old man talks to Bob, his American buddy, 'I'm closing shop Bob, come and see me.' Paul and I exchange glances. To us, his summons for Bob is not a good sign.

1 March 2007, Vallecrosia

It is cold and windy. The electronic clock outside a large pharmacy says it is 6.49 a.m. The traffic here in Italy runs on the left side in contrast to India where it runs on the right. Though I see the difference, my mind, which is stuck in a groove, finds it difficult to adapt to this change. It strikes me that if it is so difficult to let go of even such simple patterns of daily life, how will I ever let go of a pattern in which U.G. has been centre stage for thirty years. I shudder, and not because of the cold.

I walk into U.G.'s cave. I call it the 'hot room' because of the fire burning in it and all the people who fill it. U.G. is saying, 'I have never lived off the credibility and gullibility of people. I have never sold any shoddy spiritual stuff and have exploited no one. I have never given anyone any spiritual talk.' He then suddenly turns to me with a twinkle in his eyes and says, 'My daughter has got the visa.'

I look for Sid in the crowd, that warm American who was once a marine and fought one of the bloodiest battles in Vietnam. I'm told that he has left before my arrival. My old man says, 'Do you know, Mahesh, he fell at my feet and said, "I love you so much, U.G." It looks like my push to make people do what their hearts actually want them to do seems to be having an effect.'

The scene in the kitchen is strange. In the early morning, people here are talking about suicide. I am thirsting for coffee. Paul senses my urge and generously offers to fix me some. 'Whenever U.G. has to make a trip, he makes sure his bags are packed much in advance. I don't see his bags packed; he's not going anywhere,' I say. Everyone in the kitchen nods in agreement. 'He's just getting rid of all the junk,' says Lisa. I think she has summed up what we all feel in that one sentence.

Today, U.G. plans to take three steps. He stood on his feet for a moment yesterday after about four weeks of immobility. 'Friendship starts by taking seven steps together,' says Moorty quoting Kalidasa. 'When I drink water, my body vibrates, why?' U.G. asks Larry. Larry tries his best to answer but fails to satisfy. Then U.G. peeps at the diary I am scribbling on. 'You call this English?' he mocks. He has always been amused by my writing, which is in illegible capital letters with no punctuation and terrible spelling. I sense his urge to lie down. I make room for him on the couch. A picture of Al Capone, the legendary Italian gangster, sits on the wall opposite U.G.'s couch. U.G. has great admiration for thugs and gangsters. They, he says, are better than any of the religious gangsters. U.G. lies on the couch. His legs move occasionally. People sit in the room with their eyes shut. An old wooden wall clock ticks in the background. A chair squeaks, making a racket in the silence. I go out for a stroll.

'He's making a bonfire of all his old letters,' says Lisa just as I return to the villa. I rush into his cave. 'Throw them into the fire,' he says, handing over to Larry a bunch of letters from various people. According to U.G., 'All your possessions must burn before you do.' When U.G. finishes what Larry calls 'the first round', a sigh of completion escapes his lips. It resonates in the room. In the right-hand corner of the room I watch the flames consume those priceless letters which U.G. once referred to as 'letters of gold'.

Outside, I ask Paul Lynn to tell me about U.G.'s health. 'This is a long goodbye, Mahesh. This goodbye could last for two weeks, or two years, depending on whether he has cancer or not.' What I've been noticing in the old man ever since I've come to Vallecrosia is that he's neither interested in holding on to his life nor is he keen on giving it up. But one thing is certain: nobody's going to get a clear goodbye from U.G. We are summoned by U.G. He wants to take four steps. Typically, he attempts to take seven. Louis says, 'You are like John Wayne,' referring to U.G.'s physical condition as well as John Wayne's uncanny ability in his movies to overcome the impossible. Louis has been taking care of U.G. all these days and he has been doing a marvellous job. Soon, a 'praise Louis' session begins. He is easily embarrassed. All of a sudden U.G. begins to mock-wrestle Louis. Everyone in the room breaks into smiles. The air seems to be changing. 'By the time you leave, Mahesh, I will run,' says U.G., looking at me with fierce conviction. Then, settling down on to his white couch, which has begun to look more like his crib, he asks, 'Did I save Parveen from you or you from Parveen?' The question is familiar. I remember once, Vijay Anand, the director, at whose home U.G. stayed on and off for years in Mumbai, asking him the same question over lunch. This was U.G.'s reply: 'I did all that I did to save Mahesh from sinking into the abyss of madness that would have come from being alone with her. I knew he had a great potential which needed protection. That is why I gave so much of my time to wean her away from him.'

'So, did Parveen really flush your Rajneesh mala down the toilet?' asks Lisa, who was also once a 'Rajneeshite'. There are several stories about my break-up with Osho and, like all stories, each person chooses to believe the one that suits him or her the most. 'No,' I say. 'We had a lovers' quarrel about something and during the course of that fight, she pulled at my mala. As I tried to walk away, it snapped. Finally we made up, picked up the scattered black wooden beads and dumped them into the toilet together. Do you know, the breaking of the mala cost U.G. two hundred bucks?'

'Why?' asks Lisa, amused.

'Because all those sacred beads clogged up the toilet. The landlord, who was an acquaintance of U.G., ran to him and complained about it. So a sweeper had to be paid two hundred rupees to properly dispose of the beads.' The image of a person standing before a mirror continuously correcting his posture to get the 'right' image of himself flickers in my mind. How easily we twist facts to appear good, right and truthful when we relate an event.

U.G. takes Paul Lynn on over the idea of 'forever'. 'I

want to live forever. Can these doctors keep me alive forever?' he asks. 'Longer' and 'quicker': these are the operative words on which the entire medical industry is built. Ever since the dawn of time, man has put his might behind the attempt to make pleasure last longer and longer and to make pain disappear. U.G. is right—the medical technologists have failed. Dusk dissolves into night and the curtain comes down on the U.G. show for the day. Paul Arms, a likeable American, Lisa and I walk back through the deserted streets of Vallecrosia. The moon is climbing up in the sky. In a couple of days it will be full.

2 March 2007, Vallecrosia

'How was the night, U.G.?' I ask my old man on arrival. 'Better,' he replies. As I settle down, I realize that the room is already full of people. The fireplace in the corner glows. Dawn is just about to break. The distant ringing of the church bells announces the beginning of a new day. Paul Lynn is beginning to concede that all his projections about U.G.'s 'certain' end may have been wrong. U.G. is not holding on to his life nor is he pushing for the end. He is just sitting back and watching what's happening to his body like one who would sit back and watch a movie or a sunset, riveted, but unconcerned about the outcome.

'Today is the first day of the rest of your life,' says Larry Morris.

'If it is the first day, then it is also the last day of your life,' counters U.G.

'Good morning, U.G. How are you?' greets Moorty as he steps into the room.

'I feel good. I am ready to walk on my own to the bathroom today,' U.G. answers promptly. Later Paul Lynn and I sit outside in the garden in the bright sunlight and talk about the old man. 'He is a magician. He is getting better, but at the same time, he is also talking about euthanasia,' he says.

'There is no birth so how can there be death?' said U.G. a while ago. I ponder this statement. I realize that inside a mother's womb, a process which has been going on since the 'birth' of life, constantly replays. This action we read and interpret as the birth of a child and call it its beginning. Similarly, 'death' is a process which occurs within that space called 'you'. And when that occurs, it leads to the disintegration of that form called 'you'. We call this disintegration 'death'. When you interfere with this occurrence you interfere with the stream of life.

I step into the room. He is sleeping. His breathing is loud and has a rhythm of its own. The silence between the breath going in and the breath coming out is explosive. I notice little black ants dancing and playing on the white couch where he is sleeping.

'Don't hurt them. They are my best friends. They are more welcome here than all of you guys,' warned U.G. when someone wanted to kill them this morning.

He keeps a nail-cutter by his bedside. 'I cut my nails yesterday. Look, they have grown again! They grow so fast!' exclaims U.G., showing his nails to Susan. His comment lights up the room. However, he immediately says, 'Come on, my days are numbered.' A hush descends in the room. U.G. has put his finger on something we all have been dreading. And then, he gets up with the help of Louis and begins to walk in place. I begin to sing: '*When Johnny comes marching home again, hurrah, hurrah!*' Everyone in the room joins in. All of us feel like parents who have managed to get an ailing child back on his feet.

Later. 'I'm not going to go back to lead the life I've been leading for ninety years. Neither is my life from here on going to be a modified continuity of the old,' declares U.G., just when everybody around is beginning to get the bogus feeling that happy days are here again. I walk to my apartment to take a break. On the way, I call my brother Mukesh. He informs me that our unit has left for Bangkok for the shooting of *Awarapan*. Pooja is also planning to start her film *Dhoka* on the 14th of March. It's getting warm, but the winds are still gusty. A thought flashes through my head: If his life is going to change, why should my life remain the same?

Later on, I'm sitting on the lawn of the villa with Louis when a journalist from Mumbai calls to inform me that some sleazy film-maker is planning to make a film called *Parveen 'Bobby'*. He says that the film threatens to expose how I exploited her. Having said that, he asks me for my comments. 'Since it is a work of fiction no one can and no one should object to it. I will be the last person to oppose it,' I say. The journalist is disappointed. He has failed to get the kind of response he was hoping for. He tries another tactic. He begins to feign concern for Parveen. 'But sir, don't you think it's not right for him to tarnish her image, especially after she is dead?'

'How can you hurt Parveen? You cannot hurt the dead, can you?' I say. Louis, who has overheard what I've been saying, smiles.

U.G. says that the 'voice' in his head is back. 'It's telling me to "Go, go, go," Mahesh!'

I ask him, 'Go where, U.G., where does the voice want you to go?'

'It says "Go, die! You have lived for ninety years, enjoyed everything that this life had to offer. Now go!" But the only thing is, the body is not ready to go just yet.'

This brings Moorty into the discussion. 'I wonder what stops you from going,' Moorty asks.

'My body does not want to go,' repeats U.G. I can sense that Moorty is not very happy with U.G.'s reply.

Moorty throws up his hands, saying, 'It's a stalemate. He can't kill himself and he won't eat or drink anything to keep himself going. He's just withering away.' His words echo in the room and die there. U.G. does not respond. Neither do we. Outside, a pale silver moon, much bigger than the one I've seen last night, has climbed up into the evening sky.

Later, Paul Arms talks to me about how dogs, when they sense the end is near, go into a corner and die. 'What stops him from doing that?' asks Moorty.

'He has a job to finish. He still has to meet his friends,' says Paul. Moorty does not look convinced. One expects something to 'happen' by the time I leave.

Later, U.G. gets up and walks around the room. He comes up to me and shakes my hand. The sunshine is back. For how long, I wonder.

'How was the soup?' he asks as soon as I step back into his room after finishing my supper.

'Very good, but somehow I got this feeling that I have tasted this soup before. Was it Italian?' I ask, trying to recall where I last tasted such excellent soup.

'American,' says Lisa. Her reply makes U.G. smile.

Night descends and the chill returns. For the first time since U.G. has taken ill, I begin to get this uneasy feeling that the end may be close. I hope I am wrong. As I watch, the evening deepens and the quality of silence in the room changes. Most of us who are present sense that something is not quite right. The hum of the refrigerator and the sounds of the distant traffic fill the room. And then he turns towards the corner of the room where I am sitting and with a glint in his eyes says, 'Oh, there you are!' The affection with which he says these words floods the grim room with warmth. The church bells ring at a distance. And then, just when I thought the day was over, comes his parting message: 'The body does not want to live nor does it want to die. There is no birth for the body neither is there any death for the body.'

Paul Arms, Larry Morris, Susan and I stand by the shore of the noisy Mediterranean Sea sharing our views about what we think is going on in U.G.'s cave. The air is still. Nothing is making any sense.

3 March 2007, Vallecrosia

U.G.'s daughter Bulbul arrives. She is unusually calm and in total control of her emotions. She does not look like a child who has come to see a parent who may not be around for much longer. But then U.G. abandoned his kids years ago and he and his children have never really shared a parent–child relationship. 'Your past is catching up with you, U.G.,' I say to U.G. a few moments before Bulbul walks in. U.G. had tried to persuade his wife to abort Bulbul but failed in the attempt. 'My reasons were economic,' he had said. After she was born, Bulbul would often tease her father, 'Look I'm here, I'm here!'

'She must kill you now the way you once wanted to kill her,' I tell U.G. as I get up to open the door for Bulbul.

'I'm ready to be killed,' says U.G. in a matter-of-fact tone.

It's lunchtime. This place is being run by some very

efficient people. Whoever wants to pitch in drops whatever money he or she wants to in a small bottle. Then people take turns and cook the kind of food they can or want to. As a result, we have been having all kinds of great meals here: American soups, Italian pasta, Indian upma and so on.

'We have not come here just to watch him die. Each one of us has come here to get his last kick. There is something which is going on here on a very deep level which we do not see or understand,' says Larry. He seems absolutely convinced about what he's saying.

Tales of what goes on in U.G.'s cave manage to reach those who are outside. 'You missed the scene. Bulbul gave U.G. a cream massage on his feet. She wanted to put cream on his face but he stopped her from doing that.' The old man is finally responding to his daughter's need to serve him. Louis and I are summoned to watch U.G. walk. He gets up with Louis's help and does a 'tap' dance on the white embroidered carpet. Then, all of a sudden, he begins to bitch about J.K. He begins to ape the way J.K. would walk and begins marching like a soldier. However, he soon tires and lies on the couch. Bulbul washes his feet; U.G. enjoys it.

'I am not his daughter. I am his shishya,' says Bulbul.

'U.G. is back. He is enjoying the taste,' says my old man as he gulps down some watery soup, relishing it.

'Wow, happy days are here again,' I say.

'Only temporarily. Once the contact with the food is over, I cannot recall what the soup tasted like. You guys can. That's your tragedy,' he says.

And then, just like that, he gets up from his couch unassisted and begins to dance. He looks like a child showing off. Everyone in the room claps. I whistle.

'Eight-fifteen,' announces U.G. looking at the clock. 'Goodnight, sir.' The evening ends with unnerving suddenness.

4 March 2007, Vallecrosia

It's a sweet-smelling dawn. A sweeper, looking elegant in his orange uniform, is cleaning the streets. He is the only person I meet on my way to U.G.'s cave.

'He's burning more papers,' says Golda as I step into the kitchen to fix myself coffee and a croissant. It seems that the process of dismantling will happen in phases. Back home in India, people are celebrating Holi. Messages from friends, business acquaintances and absolute strangers keep beeping on my cellphone, wishing me a happy and colourful Holi.

'I believe you're burning things again!' I remark as soon as I enter.

'I am ready to be burnt myself. The carbon content created by the burning of this body will enrich the soil. That will be more useful to nature than this useless fellow called U.G. who is making all these noises. I've lived for ninety years; I'm ready to go.'

A call from Australia from the Ram Bhakts changes the atmosphere in the room. These Australians call U.G. every morning to enquire about his health. They greet him with 'Jai Shri Ram'. It is amusing to watch U.G. respond to them in the same way.

Today, after making the usual enquiries about his health, which, according to him is getting better by the day, the Australians wish U.G. a happy Holi. He does not reciprocate. He just hands the phone to Melissa who tactfully carries on the rest of the conversation and then hangs up. Louis talks about the lunar eclipse that occurred last night. The bells toll at a distance. 'Don't ask for whom they toll, they toll for thee, thee, thee,' says Louis. U.G. thanks Louis repeatedly for taking such good care of him. Louis brushes him away, embarrassed. 'I have to clean up all the financial matters with him so that there is no confusion before I go,' U.G. says, looking at me.

A short film festival begins. Someone has downloaded some short films and is now showing them on the computer. A Jesus film, a musical, which ends with Jesus being run over by a big red bus on the streets of New York sends everyone into splits. The second film is about a young boy going berserk in a food store. The kid is playing hell with his young dad, bullying him to buy him some sweets. As he gets progressively worse and begins to roll on the floor, embarrassing everyone around, a super flashes on the close-up of the troubled dad. It reads, 'Use condoms.'

It's a cold Sunday morning. I take a look at the space around me, at the way all these people are sitting around so casually and yet with so much affection for this man, watching these funny, impertinent films. This room hardly feels like one in which a sage is dying, spouting profundities as he goes away. It has subversion and a lot of irreverence. In his 'hours of death', he is mocking at all those ideas of sacredness put together by human thought. The flame is burning more fiercely now than it ever did before.

The third film has songs and poems from Bangalore, India. 'The sun that shines on the elephants and the sun that shines on the dog is the same,' sings Chandrasekhar in Telugu. He has the target of writing a hundred poems. So far, he has written sixty-five. The source of inspiration for the entire body of his work is this raging sage, U.G. Krishnamurti. U.G., throughout his life, has been surrounded by people from diverse cultures and worlds. Yet what amazes me is that he manages to connect with all of them deeply and feels completely at home with all of them. He is like water: he adapts himself to anything and everything without imposing his own form or colour on it. I'm slowly getting a hang of what the old man is saying. He cannot push the body to go, just as he cannot push the sun to set or the flower to bloom. That process is not in his or anyone's hands. Interfering with it is messing with the flow of life.

I speak with Immi, Emraan Hashmi. He is in Bangkok where a twenty-five-day shooting schedule of *Awarapan* has commenced. I brief him about his attitude in the key scenes that they have to shoot today. Immi listens intently. He's always been a keen listener. I can hear an unstated concern about my well-being coursing through his heart. Everyone at home who knows me knows how trying these times are. They have seen for themselves over the years what U.G. means to me.

The sun is out here in Vallecrosia; it's a hot Sunday morning. The church bells toll. The sound of U.G.'s breathing is loud. People sit around and watch him. Some meditate. I write. Outside, the flowers bloom and die. Time seems to crawl. The familiar sound of an ambulance racing through the streets with its blaring siren invades the room. This seems to happen often in this town. Then, after a while, the silence returns. I stretch on the floor and rest.

'My body is drying up. Something is wrong. Give me some water,' says U.G., jolting me out of my momentary rest. Larry serves U.G. his three sips of water.

'Hey, shut that door. If you want fresh air, go out,' U.G. screams at the Hungarian girl. She looks bewildered. 'Wanting to inhale fresh air is part of your sensual activity. It is better to have sex than breathe fresh air.'

I am looking for the first line for U.G.'s obituary. At the same time, I feel guilty for doing that because my mother always said that it was terrible to think such thoughts about elders. My mother loved U.G. She once said, 'How come you have been with him for so many years and nothing of him has rubbed off on you?' This infuriated me but made U.G. smile. Just a few months before she passed away, she put her dilemma before U.G., namely, whether or not she should hand over her body to a hospital for educational purposes after her demise. Her apprehension was that if she was buried according to her Muslim faith, it would create problems for the children who were married to Hindus. The world would then know to which faith she really belonged. U.G. emphatically told her not to give her body to the medical fraternity, saying, 'Whatever they find out about the human body and its intricacies ultimately lands up in the hands of those who use that know-how to destroy human life.' This resolved my mother's age-old problem and put her mind to rest. She passed away peacefully a few months later. The thought of writing U.G.'s obituary was put into my head yesterday by Moorty. It happened when suddenly, out of the blue, he began praising my writing skills before U.G. I suspect that it was actually U.G. who was using Moorty to put that seed in me. I watch U.G. from outside the cottage. He is lying on the couch surrounded by people. Most of them have their eyes shut. For a moment his eyes lock with mine. Then he slowly turns his face away. A beautiful bird begins to sing a melodious tune. At a distance, our host, the warm-faced Lucia, is ironing a bedsheet. All of a sudden, Louis storms out of the room and shuts the door behind him with a bang. I follow him to find out what made him do that. When I get close to him I notice that he is red in the face.

'What happened, Louis?' I ask.

'I am tired of dicking around doing nothing. "Don't run away! Don't run away!" he keeps saying. Well, I am getting away,' he thunders and, walking across the lawn, steps out of the villa and fades out of sight. I turn back to see Melissa's reaction. She smiles with a knowing look and walks away. I think Louis is being pushed into a corner by the old man. This was his way of fighting back. Mina the cat walks up to keep me company. My heart floats away to my daughter Shaheen who loves cats. Shaheen would have fallen in love with this ageing cat who hangs her tongue out like a dog every time she looks at you.

U.G. is praising Chandrasekhar. Chandrasekhar turned down a job offer from General Motors as he did not want to live in the US. The real reason for Chandrasekhar's spurning of the job offer was U.G. Valentine had slowed down and had to be looked after, and U.G. had already made plans to hand over the charge of this revolutionary Swiss lady to Chandrasekhar and his family, therefore this became the deciding factor for Babu.

Bulbul begins to argue with U.G. in Telugu. She's trying to prevail upon him to allow her to put some cream on his feet. Unlike yesterday, when he surrendered himself completely to her demands and let her have her way, he won't even let her touch his feet today. 'This is day two and the situation has drastically changed,' says Larry with a smile, sensing my surprise at the turnaround. U.G. describes Valentine, his old Swiss friend who played a pivotal role at a certain stage in his life, as the only revolutionary he ever met in his entire life. I wonder if this is nostalgia; a sudden, inexplicable revisiting of archives. He asks for Louis then not finding him around, demonstrates that he can stand up on his own two feet without anyone's help. Having done that, he concedes, however, that he cannot walk. His determination not to be dependent on anyone is indeed inspiring.

We have the privilege of witnessing the dignity with which U.G. is conducting his death. His life has truly been a gift for all of us. As I say this to myself, the entire town begins to resonate with the sound of the church bells, as if it was applauding me for my comment. Then he gets up and begins to show all of us how he can walk to the bathroom all by himself. He looks like a stubborn child. 'I don't want to be dependent on Louis nor anyone of your ilk. But I don't want to fall and start this dependence game all over again.' He is beginning to get that familiar edge. He is raging again. The topic is his old favourite,

J. Krishnamurti. His relentless assault on J.K. over the years has been like the persistent pounding of the ocean waves against the rocks. Moorty sits in the corner complaining, 'U.G. will expend all his energy saying all this. Then when we leave, he will collapse, exhausted.'

As the day comes to an end, U.G. asks for his rice. Turning to Louis who is now back, he says, 'So mister, we're stuck together for the next eight hours.' Louis is the only person who has been spending the nights with U.G. 'You replace one misery with another misery. Only when you die will you be free of misery,' says U.G. and begins to eat his rice from a plastic bowl. The clock ticks and I wait for him to say, 'Wrap it up!' but he just doesn't; he goes on and on attacking J. Krishnamurti. I wonder what makes him do this. I have known him for thirty years doing the same thing with the same vehemence. I glance at the clock. It is 8.10 p.m. There seems to be no end to the day so I slip out.

5 March 2007, Vallecrosia

I'm having dinner with Pervez Musharraf. It is such an honour to discuss world issues with the leader of Pakistan. I realize that this would not be possible without U.G.; I must thank him. But U.G. is dead, something tells me. A terrible feeling of finality shakes me out of sleep. It is 5 a.m. Another day has begun. The dream compels me to talk to Moorty. I need someone to share this dreadful feeling with. Moorty listens to my emotional ramblings with the tranquillity of a jnani, an enlightened being. He then tells me how he feels when he comes face to face with the thought of U.G.'s possible end. At the end of the discussion, the only thing I am left with is the burden of unexpressed gratitude towards U.G. 'If you feel I have done for you all that you think I have done and made you what you are today, then go and do to others what I have done to you,' he once said to me on one of our hundreds of car rides through the crowded streets of Mumbai. I guess the only way to shed this burden of gratitude is to ignite in people what has been ignited in oneself by this extraordinary man. 'This U.G. will leave many "saints" behind. Saints serve society more than sages do. The reflection of life is better than life,' he said to me as we watched a glorious sun set on the Palavakkam beach in Chennai. I don't know why, sitting here in Italy, as I watch the dawn break, I'm taken back to that particular moment.

'Oh, what's happening?' greets U.G. as soon as I enter the room. It is 6.50 a.m. and the room is full of people. The predominant sound in the room is of the clock ticking. Bulbul, his daughter, suddenly gets up and touches his feet. Having done that, she calls him Dakshinamurti and pleads with him to allow her to give him a bath. She is exasperated, saying if he does not yield, she will bring the water and pour it over him right where he is. As a new day breaks outside his cottage, U.G. leans back and stretching himself on the couch, says, 'Turn off the light!'

I get up to fix myself a cup of coffee. He looks at me and as I begin to slip out of the door he raises his hand and waves a hello, or maybe a goodbye. He looks frail, but very gentle. As I step out of the dark room into the bright sunlight, I realize that this image will stick in my memory forever.

I talk to Lisa about my nightmare and this immense burden of gratitude that I feel. 'You look different,' she says.

'Explain that,' I ask.

'You look lighter,' she replies and gazes at my face affectionately.

It is strange that she should say this to me because as I walked up to U.G.'s cave, I felt as if I had shed an old skin.

Bulbul says, 'U.G. won't be able to make a trip to Gstaad. He is too weak. His legs are too thin. He can't walk. What do we do?' This question is, in fact, in the heart of all those who are around him. There are no answers.

Melissa walks up to U.G. with his breakfast. 'No, not now; there's no demand for any food,' he says, shooing her away. What is peculiar about U.G. is that he eats and drinks almost nothing but he still has so much vitality and energy that he can shame all of us in this room. He suddenly begins to attack computers. 'These supercomputers are too slow and no match for the human computer. This computer explosion has only created Web maniacs.'

Louis narrates what happened at 4.30 this morning. 'U.G. tried to walk to the bathroom this morning and passed out. He was unconscious, knocked out. I can't figure out what's going on.' He has the look of a person who has seen something none of us has. Call it coincidence or call it intuition—that was the exact time I had had the bad dream. Or it could just be my Bollywood mind trying to link these two events up.

'Look, he's dying and all this is part of the dying process. He does not want to hold on to anything. All that we are doing around him is trying to make ourselves comfortable, not him. We want to hold on to him but he wants to go!' says Lisa, responding to all the talk of doing something to make the old man feel better.

Later, Lisa, Mario and I sit in the sun outside U.G.'s cave and talk. 'Express to U.G. whatever is in your hearts, don't postpone it,' is my advice to them. They get the message. Lisa says she's afraid that she will fall apart if she lets go of herself. 'Then fall apart, Lisa,' I recommend. The sun soon climbs up into the cloudless Italian sky; it gets hot.

I'm on the phone once again, talking to Immi. They're shooting the first scene between him and Ashutosh Rana. I give him the acting tips that I think he needs and hang up.

U.G. asks me to call Chandrasekhar and find out his travel plans. I do what he says. 'Enough,' he says, having listened to Chandrasekhar's story on the mobile speakerphone.

Then he talks to me about his will. 'I want to talk to you for a few minutes before you leave. When do you go?' he asks. 'On the 8th.' He nods. 'Don't you have a copy of my will?' he enquires. 'Yes, I have one in Mumbai,' I say, remembering Mukesh, with whom I have kept U.G.'s will, showing it to me a few days before I left for Italy.

When you're with U.G. you must do exactly as he says. People say that I'm totally dependent on him. On the contrary, I think that only a fiercely independent person can make the choice of leaving the most important decisions of his life in the hands of another, then live by it and face the consequences. To many this statement may seem like a paradox but to me that's the way it works.

'I'll get a bouncer and throw Julie out if she tries to push herself on me. She has to get rid of every photo, every tape she has of me and on me. I'm not the enlightened bastard you guys think I am,' he says fiercely to Paul Arms. Paul was merely passing on Julie's message. Julie had called Paul to tell him that she had put all the tapes and photos of U.G., which he wanted her to burn, in a suitcase and was ready to get rid of them.

Vennila, the Tamil lady with an American accent, asks U.G. whether she should stay or leave. She says she feels unwelcome here. U.G. tells her to leave without hesitating. 'You are not going to get anything from me or from anybody because you don't need to. How can you ask for something that you already have?' he says. Having made his point, he begins to get rid of his old documents by chucking them into the fireplace. The lady, despite being told to leave, continues to sit. U.G. does not want her to waste her time imagining she will get something from him. But, perhaps, killing false hope is love.

'He was asking for you,' says Bulbul. I step into the cave. He is lying down. After a moment, he gets up saying, 'Can I have some water?' He seems to be in pain. Louis bends forward and serves him some water. 'I just want to go into a cave and die,' he says as he sips a few drops of water from his blue mug. Of late, he has been saying this too often. Is this the cave where the end will come? Is this why we are all here? These are the questions to which there are no answers. Even U.G. cannot say what the next moment might bring. I want to sit in this cave and shower all my love on him. I want to see what miracle my love can achieve. He suddenly opens his eyes and gives me a look. His eyes look blurred. Just then Bulbul walks in, carrying her cellphone. She wants U.G. to talk to her daughter-in-law. U.G. speaks into the phone with lots of affection.

'How are my great-grandkids?' he asks.

'They want to meet you,' says the voice.

'Oh, they want to meet me? Why?' he asks, looking surprised.

'Do you want to meet them?' the voice enquires. U.G. does not reply.

I am watching him closely. Today he is in great pain. He does not show it, though. I wonder if he has cancer. 'We will never know that because U.G. will never let us find out,' says Paul Lynn before leaving.

I sit in the room opposite his and begin to summon all the energy from the world and begin to shower it on him. The feeling in the room begins to change. I feel good and U.G. falls asleep. I listen to him breathe. The clock ticks. A bird begins to chirp. The peace is suddenly shattered by the voice of U.G. saying 'Shut up, shut up, shut up!' Mario has recorded U.G.'s favourite refrain and it is now his very special ringtone. I try to recreate the blissful mood in my mind but the magic is gone.

The skies have turned grey. I can see seagulls flying back home. Night descends. I sit quietly by his side. He turns to me and asks, 'Is that Mahesh?'

'Yes, this is Mahesh,' I say. He reminds me of a toddler who is just learning to identify people with their names. After a pause he pulls himself up and sits still on his white couch. He seems to be in great pain.

'So boss!' he says, turning to Larry.

'How are you, sir?' asks Larry.

'That's an idiotic question,' says U.G., silencing him.

The day ends at 8 p.m. People slip out of his room wishing him goodnight. I leave, wishing him 'Vanakkam' in Tamil. 'Vanakkam,' he responds with the same gusto and vitality.

6 March 2007, Vallecrosia

Stealing Fires from the Gods, a book for screenwriters which explores the power of storytelling, sits on my cluttered table. My story is the journey of a man who came to U.G. to steal his fire. But instead of finding fire I discovered that U.G. had nothing but the harshest winter to offer. And it is here, in this life-threatening winter which U.G. has exposed me to, that I have discovered that deep within me there is an inextinguishable source of fire which is my own.

He is dressed differently today, all beige. 'Namaste,' I say to him. He looks good today; his face glows. 'How is it going?' he asks. Then, without pausing, he adds, 'Chandrasekhar got his Swiss visa. They're coming on Thursday morning.' With that news ends the messy visa drama which has been going on for weeks. 'I want more light,' he says, asking people to open the curtains. There is no sign of the sun and the sky is grey, cold and dull. Susan gets up to check U.G.'s pulse. According to her, today he is okay. 'He probably needs some water,' she whispers to me knowing well that any advice from a medical person will be rejected by U.G.

'Immoral bastards preach. Why do these pontiffs preach what they don't themselves practice? All ashrams are brothels. At least brothels deliver the goods. The ashrams deliver empty words and false promises. Go have your breakfast!' he suddenly barks, looking at me. With that command the first phase of the morning session ends.

I return after attending to my worldly affairs. E-mail has made life so much easier for all of us. 'Salaam Alaykum,' I say as soon as I re-enter his cave. My greeting amuses him. 'Hamid Karzai has turned against the Americans,' I say, having read about the resurgence of the Taliban in Afghanistan. After saying, 'Americans should be wiped off the face of this planet. But unfortunately, if America goes, it will take the rest of the world and all forms of life along with it,' U.G. tells Paul Arms to draw the curtains.

Paul Lynn is back from his trip. He checks U.G.'s pulse. Asked for a verdict, Paul evades. U.G. persists. So Paul tells it like it is: 'Everything is going the way it's supposed to and you're packing up.' U.G. just shrugs his shoulders. The silence is fierce; it burns one's skin. His words, said to me when I had arrived in Vallecrosia, resonate in my mind: 'I will run, Mahesh, before you leave.' He looks too frail, however, to be able to make good that promise. Even though I know nothing like it exists, I wait for a miracle to happen. I go out for a walk. It's drizzling and the weather is getting colder. I go back into the cave and join the group. Silence. The clock ticks, U.G.'s hands move like those of a dancer. I try to decipher those gestures. Kamal, a pilot with Air India, calls. He has obviously heard about U.G.'s health. Even before I ask U.G. whether he wants to talk to him, U.G. waves a clear 'no' to me. He goes out of his way to talk to an absolute stranger who just wants to say hello to him but he refuses to say even a simple hi to Kamal whom he has known for years. No one can have access to this man on the basis of their past associations.

There are two more hours before the curtains come down and people begin to leave U.G.'s cave. Tomorrow is my last day here. I sit by the feet of the master. The feet of the enlightened one have for centuries been objects of worship. U.G. has mocked and attacked that tradition all his life and I have often teased him by trying to grab his feet. I am consumed by the sound of his breathing. In the distance I hear a dog bark. He opens his eyes and stares at me. I make a face to tease him, just like I would to my kids when they were little babies. He ignores me.

He summons Paul Lynn. 'In my entire life I have never sought anyone's help to tackle my pain. You doctors have to make money by helping people cope with pain. Doctors are a menace; you need to be wiped out. I don't have an issue with dying but I don't want to repeat this kind of dependence on you guys again. This body does not need help; it can take care of itself.'

He turns to me, 'I need ten minutes to talk to you about my will. I've simplified everything, you only have to execute it.' Just before I leave, I go up to U.G. and ask him whether he would like me to come to him earlier in the morning to sort out issues. 'No need,' he says, 'we will create time to chat.'

As I lie in the dark, waiting for sleep, U.G.'s words come back to me: 'I have never been interested in making my body function in a different way. I have never done anything to free my body of pain. I have left it to the body to handle its problems by itself.' As I comprehend these words, I begin to feel like a dead leaf floating happily on a vast ocean, completely at peace with its helplessness.

7 March 2007, Vallecrosia

In his dying days my old man has filled me with the radiance of life. Here, in this quaint town by the Mediterranean Sea, I have tasted life. And now like the human heart which wants to hold on to the glory of the setting sun, the spectacle of a starlit night and the memory of sudden, unexpected love, my heart too pines to lock these memories of U.G. forever. The roads are wet, slippery and empty. I hurry to U.G.'s cave. He is lying in his familiar posture on the white couch.

'Ah, there you are. Any word from Chandrasekhar?' he asks, opening his eyes and sitting up.

'No,' I answer, settling down on the floor. The room is hot.

'I want to see you for ten minutes. That will is a complicated document. I will simplify it and tell you what needs to be done,' he says to me. I wonder why, of all the efficient people around him, he has chosen to burden me with this unnerving task. It is time for his breakfast. I have approximately fourteen more hours in his company before I take off for India.

'Come, read my pulse,' he asks Paul Lynn. U.G.'s left-side pulse, which is the governing pulse, is low today.

'You are losing weight, U.G,' says Paul, looking concerned.

'So what? Why are you doctors obsessed with losing weight and gaining weight? I don't believe there is anything to losing or gaining weight. You guys make much of it. I don't care for all that shit.' I can see that all that U.G. wants is some energy just so that he is not dependent on anyone. Paul is silent. U.G.'s body throws up all that he has eaten this morning. Melissa helps him with that. 'Sorry to bother you,' he says expressing his thankfulness.

'No bother at all, U.G.,' says Melissa sweetly. She seems humbled by his gratitude.

Morning is here. The lemon tree which keeps guard outside the glass-walled cottage peeps in, heavy with fresh new lemons. Bloom and decay are juxtaposed in this frame. 'Birth and death take place simultaneously,' says

U.G. What is bloom and what is decay? Are they just different words for change? Soni sends me a shopping list: extra virgin olive oil, ironing board cover and Black Label whisky. Work, buy, consume and die. This is the cycle we humans are trapped in.

There is more bad news from U.G.: he can't urinate. 'Let's go in and ask him what to do if he passes out,' suggests Louis. We walk into his room, Vibodha, Louis and I. Louis wants me to put the question to him. My heart skips a beat. 'U.G., we need to ask you this question: If you pass out, should people around you put you on a drip?'

'No, let me be,' he replies, shaking his hand, driving home his point loud and clear to each one of us in the room.

'And what do we do with your body when you die?' I ask.

'Throw it away in the garbage. It is more useful dead than alive.'

Then suddenly, the conversation takes a bizarre turn. 'The body does not belong to "U.G.",' he declares. 'I don't care if it stops breathing. I won't even leave behind any money for you guys to perform my funeral.' We are too affected by what he says to respond to him. Later, people sit around and begin to joke and laugh, and suggest ways of how to cope with the post-death scenario.

Louis asks, 'U.G., do we bury you or burn you?'

'I don't care.' He smilingly adds, 'But, they do say you don't burn an enlightened man.'

He gets up. 'Hey, where is that folder?' he asks Lisa.

'Which one?'

'The one with my pictures and the story of my life.' He then begins to scan through the file and starts to read aloud the names of all the books written on him in almost every language in the world.

'I am disgusted! There are four books on me in Hindi,' he says, looking at me with a twinkle in his eyes.

'Two out of four of them are my books, translated by my professor friend Jai Dixit,' I explain.

U.G. has long maintained that Hindi is a worthless language compared to Tamil and Urdu. I know that this is merely a posture.

Louis butts in. 'U.G., do you know that you have not urinated for seven hours now?'

U.G. dismisses his concern with contempt. 'Make it seven and a half hours to make it more dramatic.' All concern for him is shot down by U.G. in a similar manner.

He turns to Louis and says gleefully, 'Hey, you were asking what to do with my body. I suggest you cut it into tiny pieces and feed it to the vultures.'

Bob calls from Mumbai. He explains that he is having difficulty in getting an air ticket. 'Come before I go. I'm waiting for you, Bob,' says U.G. As he's talking, he suddenly begins to choke: he is seized with the urge to throw up what he has consumed. The conversation ends abruptly. It looks like Bob will be coming.

'What?' he asks, scrutinizing my face. He's trying to figure out what's going on in my head. '*Kuch nahin*,' I say, deliberately. This gets him going. '*Chup raho! Hindi mat boliye!*' he scolds in his heavy south Indian accent. I stop. And then I begin to say out loud the only Hindi story he can recite but I make one small alteration: I change the gender of the character. '*Ek gaon mein ek buddha rehta tha. Woh chal phir nahin sakta tha.*' He smiles and concludes what I've begun. '*Dekho purab disha mein suraj nikal raha hai.*' That's the only Hindi U.G. knows. U.G. is my sunrise.

Later I talk to Vibodha. 'What U.G. is laying out before us is a miracle,' he says.

'Yes, we'd be blind if we didn't see it. U.G. is showing us how the human body survives in such adverse conditions without even a tiny bit of support from the medical world. This is a moment of glory,' I conclude. I met U.G. thirty years ago in the high noon of his life and I've been with him through so many seasons. But this is by far the most radiant phase of his life. I feel the surge of life tearing into every pore of my being. Yes, the miracle is him.

As I jot down all that courses through my heart, Mario says, 'Mahesh, you're wanted.' I hurry into U.G.'s cave to find that jokes about disposing of his body are still circulating. U.G. is sitting up on the couch, participating in the discussion.

'Hey Louis, show Mahesh your computer,' says U.G. Louis takes out an elegant Macintosh which U.G. has gifted to him in appreciation. 'The world owes me nothing,' U.G. often said. Now he's proving this by paying back this sweet, funny American.

'It's not a question of if, but when. It may be a lot sooner, with Chandrasekhar coming in tomorrow,' says Paul Lynn, commenting on the situation. Someone replays the moments captured on camera within the cave. U.G. is watching it. He looks amused. Living through all these bizarre moments the first time is bad enough but having them played again is almost farcical. Today happens to be our German friend Mitra's fortieth birthday. Chocolate cake and Italian coffee are being served to all those who are around in the kitchen. Just next door, the old man is withering away. 'He's losing weight progressively. I wonder how he will ever be able to make it to Gstaad. He does not have the energy to go through an eight-hour drive in this condition,' says Bulbul, unable to get over her father's stubborn decision not to get any medical help. She is in anguish. But U.G. says, 'If I go, nothing is lost to mankind.' If this is not conflict, I don't know what is. I've got Soni the ironing board cover she asked for, Mario and Lisa helped me shop for it. I get back to my room and begin to pack my things. I picked up this trait from U.G.; before any journey he used to pack his bags much in advance. As I write the words 'used to', it hits me that I'm already using the past tense.

'Your one foot is already out of here,' remarked Paul earlier. This trip seems to have come to an end though something tells me that we have not come to the end of the 'end' yet. I may have to come see him again. When, why, how, I don't know.

I hear U.G. say: 'I wouldn't do anything to help anybody. You guys do all this to help me to experience your "do-gooder's high". I am not an enlightened man. You guys are doing what you are doing thinking that I am one.' Then, turning to me, he says, 'Hey, we're going to finish the job.' He then begins to explain the way to distribute the funds. Nothing he says makes any sense to me—I've never had a head for figures or for money. I guess I will have to cross the bridge when I get there. Suddenly I discover that a part of me is waiting for U.G. to mention the money that he has been saving up for me. He does not mention anything at all. I pretend it does not matter. This realization deals my absolute devotion and blind love a shattering blow. I realize the truth of what U.G. says: 'All your relationships are based on one brutal question: what can I get out of this relationship? And when you feel you can't get anything, the relationship turns into hate, apathy or indifference.' Even the guru-shishya relationship is a transactional one. What one gets out of the guru is the emotion which drives the shishya and vice versa. My insight strips me bare. Unmasked at last, I feel clean and pure in my own eyes. Perhaps this was the last scene that I was waiting for; it may be that the person I had to meet was the real me. I return to the cave lighter. The air has changed. It is 6 p.m. U.G. sleeps. I have two more hours. Seven p.m., U.G. is still sleeping. A phone call wakes him up. He asks for water. 'What's happening?' he asks, looking at me.

'You tell me.'

'I can't run.'

'But you promised me you would,' I say.

'Pas possible!' he says weakly and adds, 'I can't take the risk.' The manner in which he says it almost breaks my heart.

'What are your plans?' I ask.

'I don't know, I can't run,' he says, pointing to his withered frame.

'But you promised me you would before I left,' I insist, trying to pep him up. And then, he pulls himself up on his own two feet and begins to run on the spot looking straight into my eyes. I watch, awestruck.

'So, are you coming back again, Mahesh?' Bulbul asks.

'If he calls me, I will. I take my orders from him,' I say.

It is 7.15 p.m. I SMS Chandrasekhar who is checking in at that very moment in Mumbai airport to come here to be with U.G. The message: 'Babu, something tells me this is not the end.' A little later, I hear U.G. say the magic words to Larry: 'The pain is gone. It has been replaced by the sensation of a tickle.' Eight p.m., time to move. I wait for people to trickle out. I walk up to U.G. 'I'm leaving tomorrow morning at 4.30 a.m. Should I come see you before leaving for Nice?' I ask. 'Sure,' he says, telling me much more with his eyes. As I walk out, I hug all the folks with whom I have shared some of the most intense days of my life and bid them farewell. Moments later, walking through the deserted streets of Vallecrosia, I am seized by the certain feeling that the U.G. show is not quite over yet. Tomorrow morning will either confirm or negate my hunch.

8 March 2007, Vallecrosia

At 4.15 a.m. I am waiting outside my apartment for Mitra to pick me up and take me to U.G. before he drops me off at Nice airport. The roads are wet; it has rained again last night.

'Have you been waiting long?' asks Mitra as soon as he arrives.

'No, I have only been here a minute,' I say, getting into his plush car. The drive up to U.G.'s cave takes us hardly a minute and a half. The villa is plunged in darkness but there is light inside U.G.'s cave. I can sense that he is up and waiting for me, as always. I knock gently. Louis, who has spent the night with U.G., leaps up, signalling to me to come in. As I push open the door, I hear him say, 'U.G., Mahesh is here.' I step into the warm room. Even before I can cast my eyes on him I hear his voice. It is soft and fragile like a feather.

'Thank you, Mahesh, for all that you did for me. Thank you for coming all the way from India to see me.' His words peel the skin off my heart.

'I did nothing for you, U.G.,' I say overwhelmed more by the manner in which he is saying this than what he is saying.

'Thank you, Mitra, for driving Mahesh to the airport. It takes one and a half hours to get to Nice. What time is your flight?' he asks, being his usual meticulous self.

'Seven,' I say, sensing that the moment of parting is here. 'I don't get a sense of closure, U.G. The time for you to go is not quite here yet. What are your plans? Are you planning to go to Gstaad?'

'I don't know if I can go on this way. I am exploiting this guy,' he says, looking at Louis who is seated in the dark corner. 'He is the nicest guy. He has taken such good care of me. You are all very nice people. I cannot be a burden on him or anyone around me. This kind of life I have been leading—of people coming and sitting around me from 6 a.m. to 8 p.m.—has to stop. It cannot go on.'

I glance at Louis. I can see that he is deeply affected by the conversation.

'But U.G., dependence is a fact of life,' I say, trying to win him over.

'Man is the only creature that exploits his kind. The other forms of life don't do that.' He has torn down my philosophy of dependence.

'But this "nicest guy", Louis, has no issue in taking care of you. You have given him a computer as a gift. You can also give him that "robot" money, the money you had kept aside for "robots" to look after you.'

'Yes, if he packs me off, he can have all that money.' His riposte makes all of us smile. He is only repeating what he has been saying all along: kill me and take the money. I don't believe in the sacredness of life. You guys first destroy and kill, and then give lectures on the sanctity of life.

I glance at the clock. I sense it's time for me to leave. So I turn to U.G. and ask the question that my heart prompts me to ask: 'Do you want to tell me anything, U.G.? Do you want me to do anything?'

'Thank you for everything, Mahesh. I will see you again some day, if I'm still around,' he says, looking deep into my eyes.

'Just call me if you need me. Call me whenever you want, wherever you want.' His eyes receive my message. And then, with the finality with which one would take one's last gasp of breath, I put down my entire being at his feet.

'What are you doing? I will hit you,' he says, as if trying to stop me but actually doing nothing. His voice seems to be coming from a distance. I immerse myself completely in that moment. It's a moment of prayer, of submission, of self-annihilation. My lips kiss his feet like I have never kissed anything before. I feel washed. Then, having lived through that life-altering moment, I get up to leave. He stretches his hand affectionately in my direction to touch me. He has never done this before.

'Have a pleasant flight and, as J.K. would say, a "safe landing". That guy was always more concerned about landings.' As dawn breaks and a glorious sky lights up to usher in a brand new day over Nice, I head back home to live my life, a life which was shaped and built by a man who was to me better than any god, a man who in his hours of death gave me a taste of life.

9 March 2007, Mumbai

I'm back. It feels strange to pick up the threads of my life and step back into the business of manufacturing illusions. The old man is in my mind all the time; I call Guha to find out how U.G. is doing today.

'U.G.'s asking, how come you are not dead yet,' reports Guha with a smile in his voice. This is U.G.'s usual greeting to me, implying that with all my outspokenness, there is always someone out there waiting to get me. I feel U.G.'s warmth from five thousand miles away. 'Tell him that I cannot die till he dies,' I say. Guha repeats what I've just said to U.G. I hear Guha waiting for U.G.'s reply.

'Oh my god,' U.G. says. The conversation ends. For me, one thing is certain. I will only die when this man called U.G. dies within me for whatever I am, is him.

10 March 2007, Mumbai

For the first time since U.G. has taken ill, I get the feeling that night has set in. Suddenly, the cloud bursts within me. I break down and cry. As the night deepens, I get on the phone and call everyone who is around U.G. to get an idea of what his condition is. I sense dread and uncertainty in their voices. I toss and turn and stay awake the whole night. Finally, at 4.30 a.m., I decide to sleep. I wonder what tomorrow will bring.

11 March 2007, Mumbai

I call Guha. 'Are you in U.G.'s cave already or are you heading there?' It is 10.30 a.m. here and 6 a.m. in Italy.

'I'm here right in front of him,' he says. I feel his silence.

'How is he this morning? Is he lying down?'

'No, he's sitting up with his legs crossed.'

Then I hear him tell U.G. that it is I who is calling from India. 'Mahesh, he's asking what is it that you want to ask.' I'm relieved that he's still engaging with the world.

'Nothing, just tell him that I called to say good morning.' Guha repeats my greeting with a smile and then adds, 'He's nodding his head.'

The night has passed and the morning has brought hope. But what will tomorrow bring?

12 March 2007, Mumbai

There is a question which my heart is pushing me to ask U.G. ever since his condition became critical. I now get the opportunity to do it. 'U.G., I know you don't give a damn whether you live or die, or whether I come to see you or I don't. But I have to ask you this question: Do you want me to come back to Vallecrosia?'

Chandrasekhar, who has been with U.G. ever since I left, has turned on the speakerphone so that U.G. can listen to my voice. 'Yes,' I hear the distant answer. I then hear him tell Babu, 'Ask him to come and pack me off.' My plans to shoot *Dhoka* in Mumbai have suddenly changed. As soon as I hang up, I make arrangements to go back to Vallecrosia.

The Final Act

13 March 2007, Mumbai

My piece on U.G. and my visit to Italy is published in today's *Mid-Day*. I mail the piece to Chandrasekhar, Paul Arms and Julie. 'It's touching,' says Julie from New York over the phone. This morning, Babu read the article aloud to U.G. While he was reading, U.G. said, 'Mahesh is a good writer.' It was his only comment on the piece. He then said to Babu, 'I am just eating a little so that I can have the energy to see Mahesh.' My brother Mukesh comments on my article, 'It's a love story between the two of you,' summing up perfectly the relationship he has been a witness to for years.

Minutes before I board the flight, I check on U.G.'s condition. 'He's sitting up on his couch, quiet, with his eyes shut,' says Guha. 'I'm coming to fetch you from the airport. I want to talk to you about so many things,' says Babu, minutes before I disconnect my cellphone and head to the aircraft. As the Swiss Air flight takes off for Zurich, from where I will go to Nice and then to Vallecrosia, I realize that this is going to be the mother of all journeys for me.

14 March 2007, Zurich

It was a tough night. As my aircraft tears through the pitch-black night, covering a distance of five thousand miles, the idea of U.G.'s frail body lying stretched out there in Italy is a source of great discomfort. My plane lands in Zurich with a gentle thud. It wakes me up. The world outside looks cold and desolate. I call Babu as soon as my Indian number connects to the local network. 'U.G. called me at 5.30 a.m. He is weak and feeling some discomfort. He gave me a thousand euros to meet my expenses here in Italy. He said, "I have to hold on till Mahesh arrives."'

'Tell him to hold on, Babu. Tell him I'm coming. Tell him that I will kill him if he dares to exit from this planet without seeing me.'

I hear Babu smile. 'He will Mahesh, he will,'

My connecting flight to Nice is at 8.50 a.m. It is 7.30 now. Waiting for a flight has never been more painful. I pace impatiently through the deserted Zurich airport. I think of the conversation I had with U.G. over the phone on 1 May 2004. That was when word was going around in India that the old man was unwell and would die soon.

'Are you unwell, U.G.?'

'Very unwell,' he had said. 'I was dehydrated. I'm eighty-eight and have lived enough. I am ready to go. But, to be honest, I'm better now. Don't worry, I will see you before going. You're the only person I would like to see before I go.' His simplicity has the fragrance of love.

'So, will you call me if you feel that the time has come?' I ask.

'Yes, I will.'

'I'll drop everything I am doing and come to you,' I say.

'Thank you. I'll call you,' he repeats. The pact had been made then.

'I'm boarding the plane to Nice now. How is his condition?' I ask Guha on the phone.

'He has stopped drinking water,' says Guha. His voice sounds grim. He is almost whispering. As my tiny aircraft glides over the icy slopes of the Alps, I'm gripped by the fear that I may not be able to make it on time.

I hurry out of immigration and step into the modest Nice airport. Bob, Paul and Mario are waiting to receive me. Behind our casual facades lurks the unstated thought: when will the final moment descend on us? On the way from Nice to Vallecrosia, we talk about what has been going on. The impression that they have seen something coming of which I have no clue becomes stronger within me.

14 March 2007, Vallecrosia

The car drives up to the villa. I hurry out and head to U.G.'s cave. Even before I step in, I sense that the mood inside the cave is sombre. I find him lying on the same sofa where I had left him on the morning of the 8th. He has been lying on this sofa in this state for six weeks now. As I sit on the floor a little away from him, a teary-eyed Suguna nudges me forward, 'Talk to him.'

I call out, 'U.G.!' There is no response. Fearing that I'll never hear from him again, I reach for his feet and kiss them passionately. Tears begin to flood my eyes. Suddenly, he begins to talk.

'Thank you for coming back. You still have the power of attorney for my bank account in Switzerland. Take all the money out. Just leave the money that came to me as gifts for my birthdays in the account and then, after some time, do what you wish with the rest.'

There is no way I can, even in my wildest dreams, think of leaving him to attend to money matters, much as he wants me to. 'Babu has a problem,' I say instead, 'he wants to know what is to happen to your room in Bangalore.'

U.G. innocently asks, 'My room?' Ever since I've known

him, U.G. has never owned a place on this planet. He has always been a traveller in transit.

'Yes,' says Babu firmly, 'your room, U.G. You'd asked me to rent it for you and you said we'd talk about it later.'

'He'll probably tell you to turn it into a brothel, Babu,' I say. Everyone laughs.

U.G. just waves the subject away dismissively. Then turning to me like a concerned mother, he says, 'Go, eat something. You must be hungry.'

'Mahesh, U.G. gave me these two thousand euros to arrange for things,' says the efficient German lady, Sarito. I'm in the dining room next to the kitchen, eating something. Sarito, who was once a cab driver in Germany, has been handling U.G.'s financial affairs. Ever since I can remember, whenever I have gone to see him, the practice has been for him to take all the money on my person from me and then hand it back to me in small instalments so that I don't lose it or blow it up on useless things. But now, for the first time, the reverse seems to be happening. It makes me uneasy.

I enter the room and sit. Sanskrit chants, from a compact disc sent by Kamal and Suresh, our Air India friends, play in the background. The silence bears down on us. In order to escape it, I turn to Bob. He is leaving the next day. Using him as a ploy to draw U.G. into a conversation, I begin, 'Do you have anything to say to Bob? He's leaving tomorrow.'

'It would hurt my feelings,' U.G. answers, after a pause. Bob doesn't understand.

'He means it would hurt his feelings if he talks,' I say.

Bob says, 'I don't want you to be in any discomfort, sir.'

There is silence for a while. The silence is strangely filled with something that is rising in U.G. and is about to boil over. Suddenly, he says forcefully, 'No spiritual shit!' and then turns to me. 'What kind of a guy are you?' he asks.

I get the feeling he is trying to tell me something and I'm just not getting it. 'Tell me what you want to do, U.G.,' I ask idiotically.

'If I knew that, why would I seek your help?' he says impatiently. Everyone around laughs softly.

'Any hint?' I ask, seeking some kind of clarity.

'Just get out,' he says, with finality.

Just then, the sound of a distant ambulance siren starts somewhere and slowly fills the room. It gets louder and louder as it comes closer, becoming more and more ominous. It dawns on me that the curtains are finally coming down on the U.G. show. He wants those who have gathered here to leave and go back to wherever they came from. As people begin reluctantly to drift out of the room, confused and taken aback by the suddenness of the development, U.G. turns to me and says, 'Hey, let's get out of here!'

'Where to?'

'Anywhere.'

He looks like an irritated mother who wants her kids to leave the room and let her be. A feeling of dread begins to grow in me. I wonder what he is going to say next. Just then, Larry Morris steps in, saying, 'I'll take you anywhere you want to go.' He has probably heard what U.G. has been asking me. U.G. waves him away, irritated. 'Go away! This is not that spiritual shit! I don't have the breath to talk.' After a while, Louis steps in, making the same offer. U.G. dismisses even him. He will not be dependent on anyone any more.

Suguna and Babu, his oldest friends from Bangalore, who have been sitting quietly observing the scene, also get the message to leave. Suguna cries at U.G.'s feet. He smiles. She is filled with hope. Perhaps, she thinks to herself, she will not be among those who will be cast out.

The room is empty now. Suddenly, U.G. calls for Mitra and asks him to take a bag with his clothes and go to his apartment in Gstaad. 'Where is Shorty?' he asks, asking for Sarito. When she arrives, he asks Mitra to give her five hundred euros and asks them to leave. Mitra leaves, weeping.

And then U.G. asks me to take his passport, his most prized possession ever since I've known him, and put it in his jacket pocket. He then gestures to me to put the jacket on the chair by the door. He points to his shoes and asks me to place them under the chair. Turning to me, he again gestures to me to cut his credit card with a pair of scissors. It is time to pack up. U.G. is leaving this place just like the apartments that he lived in, ensuring he leaves no trace behind. There is no spiritual buzz around him, just pure efficiency.

'These guys have still not left. Go and tell them I will have them thrown out if they try to be clever,' he barks.

'Er . . . why don't you tell this to Babu and Suguna?' I venture, not having the heart to tell them this.

'You will say it,' he says to me fiercely. I get up to execute my master's orders.

Suguna, Babu and Bulbul are dumbstruck when they realize that they too are being asked to leave. Most of the people around leave the villa looking shocked, shattered and confused. Babu, Bulbul and Suguna step in to bid their last farewell. Bulbul weeps and speaks in Telugu, obviously pleading him to allow her to stay. U.G. doesn't relent.

Babu, sensing that the end has finally descended on him, breaks into Sanskrit shlokas and touches the feet of his master. A weepy Suguna does the same. 'This is death, Babu,' I say, as I lead him out of the room. Moments later, Louis and Melissa, who have been occupying a room in the villa, make a graceful exit, realizing that their presence would not be welcome. Silence descends on the villa. It is 6 p.m. The dance of death has now begun in earnest.

U.G. is quiet. 'Get me a wheelchair; we'll get into a car and drive away from here,' he says, making future plans.

'But I don't have a Swiss visa, U.G.'

'We can go to the south of France,' he replies. 'You get nice villas there.'

I was suddenly reminded of those days when we used to go apartment hopping in London. U.G. never liked to stay in any one place for a prolonged period.

'U.G., where will I get a wheelchair from? And I can't drive! You're forgetting that you used to take care of me; I can't take care of you in this condition,' I say, shooting down his plans even before they begin to take root.

He changes course. 'Call Larry Morris,' he says. I immediately swing into action, realizing that I have Susan's cell number saved on my mobile. She was my contact point while I was away in Mumbai. 'Come back, Larry, the old man is asking for you.' Larry and Susan, who were heading out of Vallecrosia, are taken aback by this sudden turn of events. When Larry arrives, U.G. speaks his mind and explains to him that he wants a quiet exit without so many people hanging around. He does not want the so-called 'followers' to convert his passing into a spectacle and give spiritual interpretations to it. A simple, quiet and private death of his choice is what he wants. I am here to provide such a death, assisted by Larry and Susan. I realize that finally, the role of my life is about to be played. A man who has had the courage to stand alone and live life on his own terms trusts me with his death.

15 March 2007, Vallecrosia

A loud thud jolts me out of sleep. I rush to the door to find Susan sprawled on the floor. I hurry to give her a hand.

'I slipped and fell. I wonder if all is well with U.G. It's 4.30 a.m. now. This is the exact time he had a fall before he fell ill,' she says and cautiously walks down the slippery wooden staircase to check on him. I dash back into my tiny room to change and hurry down. As soon as I reach U.G.'s cave, I see Susan stepping out. She looks calm. 'All is fine with him,' she says and heads back to her room.

I step into U.G.'s cave to relieve Larry. He has been up and keeping an eye on U.G. all night. Louis was handling this earlier but for some strange reason, U.G. suddenly asked him to leave. Larry, Susan and I have decided to take turns, making sure that U.G. is never left alone. I lie down on the floor next to him.

At dawn, Louis arrives outside the door. He looks agitated. As I step out into the cold morning, an otherwise tranquil and funny Louis seems to be in great turmoil. He unburdens his heart. I listen to him. I am moved by the simplicity and courage with which he expresses what has been bottled up inside his heart for years. Then, having released his pent-up emotion, he announces that he's leaving Vallecrosia and heading for Gstaad, Switzerland, with Melissa. As I watch him head to his room to pack his bags and leave, I realize that everyone has come here to die their own little deaths. As the morning advances, Babu and Suguna, who have come to terms with 'the end', summon me outside the villa to bid me goodbye.

It feels unusually peaceful to be sitting around U.G. Susan says his heart almost stopped beating. I look at him. He looks back; there seems to be nobody in there. When I watch him closely, I realize that he is not holding on to anything. He suddenly says, 'You got my birthday money? Take all the money out and enjoy.' Then turning to Larry and me, he says, 'Get me out of these trousers and this shirt. You want me to die in these rough clothes?' His chiding makes us smile. He continues, 'The body will go today—that is, after I go and shit. That's the great Indian tradition.'

As he shuts his eyes, I feel that we have reached the end. The countdown has begun. I suddenly recall that today also happens to be my youngest daughter Alia's fourteenth birthday. U.G. has prophesized that she will have great potential as an actress. His mouth is shut and his breathing is getting lighter. I cough to get him to respond. His toe moves and so do his fingers. Someone is still there in that body. He is breathing from the bottom of his lungs. It is getting very quiet and the room is beginning to feel empty. I send Alia an SMS, wishing her happy birthday. Her response is mature. I'm moved. Everyone—Soni, Shaheen and Alia—has been hit by the manifestation of this inevitable truth. I slip out of the room to make a brief call to Alia. She is delighted to hear my voice. I return to find that U.G.'s eyes are open. I wait to hear from him but he does not say a word. He just shuts his eyes once again and walks away to some place within himself.

Just then I get an SMS from Julie. She is in a bad state; full of regret and guilt. I suddenly notice that he's awake. I'm happy to have him back in the land of the living. I send him a passionate flying kiss. He responds and gestures to me to sit down. I do what he says. I always have. He is staring into space now. I wonder what is going on in his mind. His eyes are still, like stones, with just a little movement. The room is getting frighteningly quiet. He then looks up and waves goodbye to someone or something. And then, after staring in the same spot fiercely for a long time, he shuts his eyes and returns to his inner world once again.

An SMS from Frank Noronha, my bureaucrat friend from Bangalore, arrives: 'Bhubaneswar Nadi says that you are with U.G. in his final hours in the capacity of his son. U.G.'s friends are asking for your telephone number. Should I give it to them or not?' I promptly ask him not to. My job is to see that no one enters this space by any means or through any route. 'You're not just a bouncer whom he has summoned here to keep the world away. You're also his son,' says Susan. 'A while ago, you were eyeing his shoes. That's a son's trait, wanting to step into his father's shoes.' I am touched by the simplicity of her statement. I guess I now have a human reference point for the enormous love I feel for U.G.

My brother Mukesh calls from Bangkok. 'You must remember to carry his ashes back to India to immerse them in the Ganga,' he tells me. I see where he's coming from. He and I have become so different over the years. Mukesh has always drawn comfort from tradition and rituals. 'The Ganga is too polluted and unworthy of bearing the ashes of this extraordinarily ordinary man,' I reply. My brother is rendered speechless.

Then, Babu calls. He is about to enter Switzerland by road. I inform him about U.G.'s condition and what he said about today being the last day. He listens in deep silence. I can sense that he is now completely reconciled with the idea of U.G.'s death. He then tells me to bring up the question of his ticket money with U.G. if I get the chance. I say I will if I find it right to do so.

The day passes. U.G.'s prophesy does not come true.

16 March 2007, Vallecrosia

It's 2 a.m. I am down in U.G.'s room. The ticking of the clock seems loud. I can't hear him breathe. This hour is said to be the hour of the wolf. Madness erupts, crimes of passion, murders and suicides take place. It is also the hour when the ailing die or their pain touches its zenith. Susan is apprehensive about what 4 a.m. might bring. She simply cannot get over the fact that he fell down and hurt himself around this time of the morning.

It's 3 a.m. now. My attention is held by the grace and movement of the flames in the fireplace. Everything else within the room is still. Waiting for death is like waiting for the sun to rise. One cannot hit the fast forward button and make things move faster or slow time. Death will happen when it happens. I stand close to U.G. and watch him breathe. He feels my presence and opens his eyes. His eyes recognize me. I smile and wave to him. He then turns on his side and once again shuts his eyes. I come to the kitchen and fix myself a cup of black coffee and chew on a piece of dry bread. The hands of the clock inch towards 4 a.m.

Just as I finish putting my thoughts on paper, I see him get up suddenly to his feet in one smooth movement. He stands there for a moment suspended in time. I shout his name and dart forward, just as Larry, who is supposed to be the one keeping a watch but is snoring, wakes up with a start. Before I can do anything, U.G. tries to move. The carpet under his feet slips and he falls. My outstretched hand manages to break the fall. He lies on the ground on his side while Larry and I, who have rushed towards him, now stand rooted to the spot, frozen with shock, horror and shame.

'Pick me up,' U.G. says in a complaining tone. We place his frail body on the sofa and help him sit. The fall was light, given his body weight.

'Are you hurt?' asks Larry anxiously.

'No,' answers U.G., shaking his head.

I glance at the clock. It's 4.25 a.m. Susan's fears have come true.

'Where is Susan?' U.G. asks.

'Shall I call her?' asks Larry.

No, he signals impatiently, 'I was just asking . . .' I wonder what the repercussions of this fall might be. Larry sits on the sofa, filled with remorse. His words, 'Pick me up,' echo in my head. To see a man like him in a situation like this is painful. A voice in my head says, 'I hope he goes soon.' If it was not looked upon as a crime and if U.G. asked me to, I would not have hesitated to help him make the exit. The moment I think this, I'm shocked at the thoughts coursing through my heart.

He opens his eyes and asks for a sip of water. Then, turning to Susan, he says, 'What about your lunch?' Even in the throes of death, he cares about the needs of others. I sit in the cave listening to the music of his breathing. It seems to me that the memory of this elemental activity of life will displace the memory of all the conversations I have had with him over the last thirty years.

'His breathing is much weaker,' says Susan. Outside our window, I notice that dawn has broken. He sits up suddenly. I am ready for him this time so I dart forward and block his path, making sure that what happened earlier this morning doesn't repeat itself. He wants to go to the toilet. I scream out to Larry for help. He races into the room and takes charge. Susan and I are worried about what will happen next. U.G. looks like a leaf trembling on a branch, waiting for a strong gust of wind to blow him away. Immi calls me from Bangkok. Today they are shooting the key scene of *Awarapan*. Briefing an actor from someone's deathbed is not something I ever thought I would be able to do.

Louis and Melissa make their final exit from the villa with grace and dignity. I tell Louis what U.G. told me in 1979 when he put me in an autorickshaw in Bangalore, 'When you look back on this day, you will realize that this is the happiest day of your life. Go, Mahesh, you're done. A new chapter in your life has begun.'

Bulbul, who is still around somewhere in Nice, feels that U.G. will live through this. She says she does not want to go back to India. Even if she does, she says, she will only go to come back. She says with great conviction that she is destined to take care of him.

U.G. turns to me and looking straight into my eyes, asks, 'When is your ticket? You cannot leave today.'

'I have an open ticket, sir,' I reply.

'It'll take a few days for me to go. Just handle this well . . .'

U.G. is entrusting to me an almost impossibly difficult task in the same manner in which he would ask me to arrange for tickets or visas. A couple of years ago, in London, the fog played havoc with all flight schedules. I had made reservations for myself to go to Mumbai and for U.G. to travel to New York. My seat was confirmed, U.G.'s was yet to be. When I was packing my things to leave London without managing to get a confirmation for U.G., he said, 'If you don't get me out of this fog, I won't let you go. I will chain you to that chair and keep you here with me.' Today, I have to see U.G. out of this fog.

Ever since U.G. spoke to me about organizing the 'end', it seems as if one has caught a glimpse of the light at the end of a long, dark tunnel. When I walk into my room and check my air ticket, I get the shock of my life. It says that I'm supposed to fly out tomorrow! But what dawns on me is far more awesome: this dying old man lying there on his couch knew something I did not. Or am I just seeing something in nothing?

I see now that he is in discomfort. Wanting to lessen his discomfort in some way, I try to blow some kisses at him. He waves back, signalling, 'Don't do that.' Making any kind of contact seems to hurt him. Love is a frill he can do without. No food, no water, no love, nothing—he wants nothing. Then what is it that keeps him here, I wonder?

I step out into the lawn and call Mukunda Rao, the

sweet, gentle savant from Bangalore. I ask him to write U.G.'s obituary and keep it ready. I tell him I will fill him in with further details when the death actually occurs. 'I know U.G. doesn't give a damn but the world needs to know of the exit of such a man,' I tell him.

Four thousand euros is all that we have to take care of U.G.'s cremation. Of course, lots more can always pour in to make his funeral a grand affair. But since I have been given the charge of disposing of his body, I will insist, as U.G. would, that no frills are to be added to his cremation. Sitting next to U.G., I feel I'm sitting near a flame that has become cool and gentle. There is lightness in the air. Just then my cellphone beeps. It is Soni who is messaging to tell me about Musharraf trying to gag Geo TV in Pakistan. A man would die to try and hold on to power. And here, in this room, lies a man who himself turned his back on power but never said a word against others pursuing it.

U.G. is very frail and needs to be helped even to sit up. He ingests no food or water but still goes on. The human body is an incredible powerhouse. As he sits up, overpowering energy gushes into the room. U.G. signals to Larry but he cannot understand what U.G. is trying to say. So, making an impatient gesture, U.G. disconnects all communication with us. Sarito messages: 'I have information for you. Meet me outside.' I hurry into the cold. On my way out I meet Lucia who is our hostess and the owner of this gorgeous villa. We discuss the post-death scenario. According to Sarito, 'You have to keep the body here for twenty-four hours before you can cremate it. A law officer and a doctor will come and certify that there has been no foul play and that will be it. But you need a letter from U.G. giving you the authority to cremate him.'

I ask U.G. for the letter of authority. He listens and gestures, 'Bring it to me, I'll sign it.' The letter is drafted and printed with the help of these two efficient ladies, Sarito and Lucia. I walk down with his favourite red pen, with which he has signed so many documents in the past, to get his signature on this last and final testament. I enter the room and tell him that the letter is ready. I point to the spot where he needs to sign. He puts his distinctive signature, with the three dots, his trademark, with a flourish, without showing any emotion or even reading the contents. Then he turns towards the fireplace and makes a gesture that looks like a swaha, almost as if he is offering himself to the fire. 'Thank you,' I whisper to him and walk out of the room.

17 March 2007, Vallecrosia

One a.m. It was a restless night. I am in the room next to U.G.'s. He is sleeping on his side, with the clock on a small side table sitting right next to his face. His breathing is getting shallow. We are approaching 4.30, a dangerous hour for U.G. Larry has asked me to wake him up at 4.15 so that he can watch U.G.

The birds in the garden begin to sing. U.G. has been rather still for the last hour. Susan walks in, a little earlier than scheduled. 'Something has changed in this room,' she says. We wait to see if he will wake up at 4.30 a.m. This is the time at which he has been waking up for years. We decide that if U.G. does not wake up, we will pinch his foot. If he does not respond, we will leave him like that. He has always made it known that he doesn't want to be plugged into any life-support system. I send a reply to Soni, who had SMS'd me to find out how U.G. is: 'He gave me the status of a son; he wants me to cremate him and see that I don't let anyone know where his ashes are dumped. I have to fight all my life to see that I don't let him become a god.'

He stirs. Someone has come back home. Sitting here in this room feels as if I'm sitting on the seashore next to a receding ocean. There is a tired but fulfilled sound. I go out and return to the cave after some time. 'His breath has slowed down. I would say his condition is critical now. Look, he's looking darker. There is less oxygen in his body,' reports Susan. His body shifts position. Just when you think he's done, he moves a hand or foot to say it's not over yet. Pooja calls to find out how things are with me in Vallecrosia. She has written in her *Mid-Day* column about U.G. She talks about her memories of U.G.

in San Francisco. She was seventeen then. Her voice has a trace of pain.

High noon. The church bells are ringing in the distance. He makes a sudden movement and then begins to make gestures as if he is conversing with someone. He is questioning, quarrelling with this invisible entity. I watch him and then watch Susan looking at him like a mother. She is moved and wonderstruck. I go out.

'He threw the towel at me,' Larry says to me when I return. Susan is smiling. One can sense the joy held back in Larry's voice. Susan, who has witnessed it, re-enacts the manner in which U.G. threw the towel. 'He's fed up with covering himself,' says Susan, referring to U.G.'s habit of constantly making sure that he was properly covered to avoid any embarrassment.

Discarding these social niceties can be a terrifying experience to behold, especially when the final layer that is discarded is the 'self', or that persona I have come to identify as 'U.G.' And, with that final layer, goes not only the person but everything that is perceived as 'sacred', or 'enlightened', about the person. Early that evening, as I sat in U.G.'s room, he made a move to get up to his feet. I darted to him and blocked any possibility of movement. I had barely uttered the words, 'You want something, U.G.?' when I saw his face. What was looking back at me didn't look anything like U.G.—it was more some kind of prehistoric animal. His eyes, with no memory, did not look human. And then this beast spoke. Guttural sounds spewed forth, almost as if the sounds were not coming out but going inwards. Bewildered, still staring at the creature before me, I screamed out to Larry. By the time he came in, the creature had disappeared and U.G. had returned. He wanted to pee. I handed over charge to Larry and rushed out into the cold night.

18 March 2007, Vallecrosia

'Call. Urgent,' says a message from Mukesh. It is 2 a.m. here in Italy and 8.30 a.m. in Bangkok. When I call them I find that they want me to clarify a key dialogue in the last scene of *Awarapan*. Then Larry speaks his heart out to me. He explains that Susan, he and I being here in this crucial phase of U.G.'s life means a lot more to him than he demonstrates. He tells me to feel free to lean on him in any way if I feel the need. I kiss his hand and thank him for his generosity.

I lie on the floor next to U.G.; there is no one else in the room. Unless I tell myself that he is dying, nothing from the expression on his face indicates that he is going to. His hands move. I wonder what the next hour will bring. I feel light and free, as if a prison inside me which had kept me caged from the time I was born has melted away. Later, when I tell Susan about the experience with U.G. last night, she explains that it was a seizure. I explain to her that all I am left with from the experience is a sense of love and deep trust.

It is 4.30 a.m. again, the hour when U.G. is most vulnerable. As soon as I write these words, it strikes me that only those who want to preserve themselves, or keep what they have going, guard themselves from vulnerabilities. If U.G. is not interested in holding on, what is the point of anybody guarding him? All our structures of thought and all the institutions that man has created over time are built on the basic impulse of preserving things forever.

Soon, morning arrives, without incident. I walk up and down the lawn. Mina, the old cat, who is actually the true resident of this place, walks along with me. She seems to like me. I am invaded by a feeling of certainty that I am in the right place doing what destiny has willed for me. Keeping guard outside the villa while my master waits for death is the role I was born to play in this relationship. The thought strikes me that perhaps I can make a film based on these days—the last film that I would ever direct. I wonder if this plan will materialize. Perhaps not.

I step back into the room. It is abnormally still. Larry and I talk in the kitchen over coffee. He expresses his deep gratitude to U.G. for saving his life. While he narrates the story of how he was saved by U.G. from a near-death experience a few years ago, he begins to choke with emotion. I tell him, 'You need to do that more often,

Larry. Don't you know, the burden of unexpressed gratitude is a difficult cross to bear?'

Suddenly, with Soni's call, the tone of the day changes. She is worried about the repercussions of not getting medical help for U.G. 'It is illegal in the West to do what you guys are doing,' she says with great concern in her voice. I put her fears to rest by assuring her that all that needs to be done has been looked into by my host here. I get a message from Louis wanting to talk to me about some issue. He is obviously having second thoughts on the question of money. It's too late now; U.G. is not talking. He barely manages to say a word to communicate his toilet needs. For the first time since I've come here, I sleep in the afternoon. Perhaps it's the new moon that is affecting us all. Even U.G. is very quiet but he continues to make those familiar swaha gestures as if he is discarding parts of himself.

It's getting dark inside the cave now. Frank messages, asking about U.G.'s condition. I don't reply. Nothing must come into the silence of this place. 'Life is fire. It burns anything that is dead,' U.G. had once said to me, way back in the 1980s. I find his words in operation right here in front of my eyes. U.G.'s body is feeding on itself, just like fire does. 'Watch him burn like you would watch a fire burn and burn itself out, Susan. Just feel the glow,' I say.

19 March 2007, Vallecrosia

Five minutes past 5 a.m., and a new dawn is about to be born. It is a blessing to witness the glory of this man who lived and now dies on his own terms. Suddenly, I cry. I am grateful for these tears which help me to cope with this inferno that has engulfed me.

'Larry feels you should come in for a while and have a look at U.G. He feels he might suddenly crash,' says Susan, walking into the kitchen where I'm having my coffee. I empty my cup into the sink and head towards the cave. The wind is blowing strongly. As I enter the room, I discover that the sound of the clock is louder than the sound of his breath. He is still making those strange swaha-like gestures. He looks at me and his eyes call out to me. I hurry and get close to him. He brings his hands together and does a pranam. Every pore of his being seems to be saying 'thank you'. Is this a farewell?

Eight-thirty a.m., the fireplace is still alive. I sit here listening to the music of his breath. The birds chirp outside. The sound of traffic says that while U.G. goes through the throes of death, it's just another day out there in the world. The room is beginning to feel lighter and lighter. U.G. turns to Larry who hurriedly moves towards him. He gestures to Larry to sit. He then starts to pull his hair over his face in a very childlike, cute fashion. These are the most intimate times that I have ever spent with U.G. Then he looks at me fondly and makes the same swaha gesture, as if offering me to the fire. He is now turning away from me. I smile and say a heartfelt goodbye to him. Strangely, it does not hurt to do that. Those who gave birth to the idea of permanence are the real enemies of mankind.

Death takes a long time to come. His body has shrivelled up. It looks like the body of someone who is the victim of severe famine. But the only thing that keeps occurring to me is that while those in a famine situation have no choice, here it is U.G. who is presiding over this process. I cancel my reservation for my return trip to India. I have the most important task at hand to attend to here: I have to cremate U.G.'s body and rest his ashes in a place which no one can ever find. Life will have to take a pause for death.

Larry is trying to talk to U.G. I decide to step in to see if I can help. When I get close, I see a look which I have never seen on his face all through this illness. He is just staring and his eyes don't show any trace of recognition. 'Get Susan, we're losing him,' says Larry, trying to suppress a sob. I rush out to fetch her. Unlike Larry, she, being a doctor, is very calm. We place him flat on his back. He breathes. Larry begins to weep. The sun seems to have set. What is left is the afterglow. U.G. looks off and on with great urgency in my direction. I wonder if he wants to say something. I go out to message Soni. She is holidaying in Jodhpur with her sister who is visiting from

Geneva. I enter the cave again. U.G. looks at me and signals to me to sit close to him. I hurry forward and sit down. He keeps looking at me; I smile at him. He looks at me closely, as if to find out how I'm dealing with his going away. I feel all right and I know he sees that in my face. U.G. is forcing me to look at this process of death up close and in slow motion. It feels as if I am watching a big, orange sun slowly dip into a huge ocean.

20 March 2007, Vallecrosia

The crackling of the fire, the ticking of the clock and U.G.'s accelerated breathing are my only companions as we approach the hour of the wolf. It is 2 a.m. and my shift begins now. These are the most important moments of my relationship with U.G. I sit here asking myself a fundamental question: What is it that I want? Do I want him to live or do I want him to go? 'Go' is the answer. I want what he wants. The rough, brittle edges of life seem to have smoothened out and I feel an all-pervasive feeling of gentleness. The room no longer feels like an inferno one wants to escape from. It feels more like the cool shade of a tree.

Three-forty a.m. I pull myself away from the door of sleep and begin to write furiously. I'm lying on the floor very close to him, just like I would whenever I lived with him. I realize that the feeling must write itself. You cannot write to evoke a feeling. I then go out for a shower. When I come back, U.G. seems to be in distress. He is tossing and turning his head and is gasping for breath. I go close to him. He looks at me and once again signals to me to sit. As always, I do what he says. As I sit, I am reminded of a conversation I had with U.G. a couple of years ago. He jokingly said, 'Mahesh, it is for future historians to figure out whether I made you famous or you made me famous.' His laughter reverberates in my head.

I go out to the kitchen for breakfast; the most delicious I've had in my entire life. On the table sit two Italian croissants. Ever since I've come to this place, the abnormal rhythm of our life has forced us to eat leftovers and dry pieces of stale bread. Susan has taken the initiative and changed the menu in the 'death ward'. The big Italian croissant has marmalade in it. U.G. has not eaten a grain for nine days. What must be going on in that body which lies stretched before my eyes gasping for breath? Mario calls to say that the crematorium will need U.G.'s will. I tell him to ask Mitra to come back from Gstaad with the will. I also instruct Mario not to tell anyone what is going on inside the villa. I must demolish the illusion that this is some kind of an ashram and I'm here to give people updates from time to time about 'guruji's' health.

U.G. is trying to make signs again. I call out to Larry to see if he can understand what U.G. is saying. Nobody can. Then he gestures to me to sit down, and I, bewildered, watch him. I reach forward and gently touch his foot. It feels cool but responds to my touch. 'The blood goes to the core of the body,' says Susan, explaining why his feet feel cool. It is 4.15 a.m., that dreaded hour. Nothing happens, though. Susan asks, 'Do you know why we feel so protective towards the dying and the very young?' I don't. She explains, 'It is because this instinct has been hard-wired into the human race for self-preservation.' Having Susan here with us is a great help. She has dealt with the painful illness of her son who was incapacitated for years. She knows how to watch over a person who is in a fragile state. But the basic difference between her past situation and this one is that here, none of us is supposed to hold on to the old man and prevent him from going.

I am in my bedroom and Susan, as she heads towards the attached bathroom, says, 'He is shifting and turning in a weird way.' I head downstairs and enter the cave. Larry suggests that I should not keep Mario in the loop about what's happening in the cave. 'He will call and tell everyone and we will have a problem here,' he says, getting up and heading for the door.

Later, the air in the room is full of laughter. Larry and Susan are laughing and talking about their marriage and how U.G. gave Larry the green light to tie the knot. Larry talks about the trip to London that U.G. and he were supposed to make; it never happened. I suggest to him that they should make it now. The idea seems attractive to him. It's getting cold. 'These are the winds from the Arctic blowing over the mountains,' says Lucia, our charming, warm-hearted hostess. She shoots down Larry's suggestion that Mario should not be told about what's going on here. I step in and resolve the issue by suggesting that even if Mario tells people about what's happening, I would make sure there would be no one else to play a part in the last scene.

'He looks like any old man dying in a nursing care unit,' says Susan.

'Oh, he would love to hear this coming from you, Susan,' I say. U.G. always liked being told he is ordinary, unlike the rest of us who want to be told the opposite all the time.

Something prompts me to talk to the Indian consulate in Rome, just to get an idea of the cremation procedure for an Indian national in Italy. 'You need a clearance for the cremation,' says the consul general, sounding very courteous and gentle. He was rather prompt in coming on the line. My name seems to have the power to unlock doors now. The consul general gives me a number in Milan to speed things up. 'They will guide you,' he says. When I fail to get a response from the number in Milan, I call Ravi Shankar, the personal assistant to E. Ahmed, minister of state for foreign affairs, to seek his assistance. 'I will talk to these people tomorrow,' says Ravi who has already been very helpful.

Lucia says that the mortuary attendants have informed her that they do not need the letter from the Indian consulate. 'Since you don't want to take the ashes back to India, the Indian laws do not apply here in Italy,' she adds emphatically. I speak to Ravi Thapar in the Indian consulate in Milan. Ravi is taken aback by my wanting to expedite the bureaucratic procedure in anticipation of U.G.'s death. 'These matters of birth and death are not in the hands of us mortals. We can't predict them,' he says, explaining his point of view. However, he promises to call me back within an hour to explain to me what needs to be done to arrange for a smooth cremation. U.G.'s breathing is very weak now. If he makes it through the night, it will be a miracle.

I get a call from the Indian consulate in Milan. It's Ravi Thapar again. I can see that the Indian consulate, and he in particular, are extending themselves to help me tide over this situation. In the last one hour, he has read three chapters of my biography on U.G. which he found on the internet. 'U.G. is very bold in his expression. And your writing comes straight from your heart,' he says, sounding strikingly reverential in his tone. What baffles him is that I'm not taking U.G.'s ashes back to India. As we hang up, he says he will call me in case he needs the letter that U.G. has given to authorize his own cremation.

The temperature is plummeting. I seek Lucia's help to turn on the central heating of the villa. 'We need to warm up this house. It's going to be a long, cold night,' says Susan while attending to business relating to their church in Albuquerque over the phone. I've got to know this quiet, soft woman in the last four days better than I ever did in the last sixteen years.

Larry and I go to the kitchen to attend to business. The pressures of our respective professions are beginning to assert themselves in this distant town of Vallecrosia, despite our reluctance. I bet U.G. would be very happy to see us doing this. He always pushed people away from him into the world and commended them whenever they made a mark for themselves.

I step back into the cave. It's dark. I switch on the light. The scene is familiar: U.G. lies on the sofa and Susan sits with her eyes shut. Mario calls, 'Mitra has come with U.G.'s will.'

'Bring it to me now,' I tell him and head straight out of the room to the back entrance of the villa to meet him. As soon as Mario gets out of the car, I notice that he has an uncertain and harassed air about him. 'How is U.G.?' he asks, unable to keep the question to himself. I give him the picture. He listens very intently and asks, looking at me with great concern, 'Are you okay?' I smile.

I read the will. I feel like I did on my first day at school—I understand nothing. Susan tries her best to explain it to me. Larry joins in and succeeds in making me understand some points. Seeing that I'm still quite clueless, he smiles affectionately and offers me all his help in sorting out these matters. As the day slips into night, talk of money eclipses the issues of death.

21 March 2007, Vallecrosia

'Mahesh!' Larry calls. I leap out of bed and head to the living room where U.G. is. 'He has stopped moving his head. I think we are there. Can we call Susan?' he says, sounding unusually calm. I dart into the cold night, then head up the narrow, slippery wooden stairway and call out to Susan. 'Coming,' she answers. We all assemble in the room and find that his breathing is very shallow. He is at the threshold but not there yet. The wait continues. Today ends the seventh week of U.G.'s stay in Vallecrosia. Larry enchants us with his stories of the time he spent in the army in Alaska and Korea.

Three a.m.; U.G. is still in the land of the living though he breathes slowly. I go out to change my trousers and wash the shirt I've been wearing for days in the tiny bathroom sink. Then I catch a short nap and return to U.G.'s cave. 'Same,' says Susan. 'No change.' I watch him for a while and then get up. Before I go out, I touch U.G.'s feet to see how they respond to my touch. They are cold and dead. The big toe, though, still feels soft. 'There is no response to my touch,' I say to Susan.

'You think he's dying?'

'I think so,' I say, and then, bending down, kiss his cold feet gently and walk out into the new morning. The storm has passed. Mina the cat runs up to me. Overwhelmed, I bend down to pat and stroke her, this time, for a bit longer. I don't know why, but I feel the need to love life today. It is 10.24 a.m. The sun is out. It makes every blade of grass, which still holds the morning dewdrops, glitter. Soni is in Udaipur. I inform her of the scene here. Her SMS reveals how severely she has been hit by the unusual manner in which U.G. is saying goodbye to the world. 'What a process it is to die! And what a strong life force which still persists in a man who does not want to live! I can't understand it. And I can't imagine how trying it must be for you who are normally so restless, to wait patiently for your friend to leave. I'm very moved by it all,' she writes.

'When it comes to devotion, there is no choice involved. People think there is a choice in operation but that is not correct,' says Larry Morris. I agree with him. Just as one cannot claim credit for the body one possesses, one cannot boast of the devotion one feels towards another.

Ravi Thapar calls up to clarify a few details. Later, Lucia, Mario, Sarito and I walk to the city office to check if they need any more documents to cremate my old man. The city office is a quiet place and the official in charge is an efficient man. He is brief and clear and puts all our fears to rest saying that we have all the papers we need. As we step out into the street, I realize that I've not been out of the villa for seven days. 'How does it feel?' asks Sarito when she learns about this.

'The world looks unreal,' I tell her.

'You look good,' says Mario, praising me for the task I'm doing. 'I better do it well, Mario; this is the most important job of my life,' I say, meaning every word.

When we get back to the villa, Susan informs us that the cave was attacked by thousands of ants. 'They're coming to party on U.G.'s body,' I say, remembering what he had once said. 'When death occurs, or is about to occur, the ants are the first to know.' The body is immortal; it contributes to the continuity of life even after death. U.G.'s words are being confirmed by his own life. U.G. told us a few days ago: All that is here is a breathing, pulsating body, a feeling of weightless form. When the breathing stops that is when you will say death has occurred. Thereafter, what to do with this form will be your problem. There is no fear, no interest in me to stop death or keep this body going.

22 March 2007, Vallecrosia

U.G.'s movements are getting less and less noticeable and frequent. I get the feeling that he's simply sliding into the arms of death. Susan enters at 3.50 a.m. She has been doing this with great precision for the last seven days. Even before she settles down she enquires how he is. I give her my update. We sit in the room, held by the silence. And then, Susan sighs, a sound that reverberates through the room. It is the most eloquent expression of what we all have been feeling for the past so many days. It is 5.00 a.m. now. The smell of coffee, of which Susan has brought me a cup, is divine. I sip the coffee and watch my best friend die. Outside, the sun is out, but it is still very cold.

At 8.15 a.m. Susan screams, 'Oh my god, Mahesh, look, ants!' I turn. Thousands of black ants have marched in line along the white carpet, up the white sofa and on to U.G.'s stone-like face where they have finally spread out, darkening the left side of his face completely. As we move closer, we see that there is an intensity of life about them, in contrast to U.G.'s intense calm. 'Larry,' I scream, realizing that we need more help. We all have to exercise great calm and get the ants, which U.G. always called his friends, off his face.

Susan uses the ant-repellent spray. She bought this eco-friendly spray only the other day; little did we know that it would be put to use so soon. After a great struggle, we get the ants off U.G. Thereafter, Susan uses her doctor's dexterity to change the sheets U.G. is lying on. 'Normalcy' returns. Why the ants went straight for U.G. with all of us keeping watch is the unasked question that bothers us all.

Larry explains: 'They come when you're still. They used to crawl on me when I meditated here in this room.'

'Unless man comes to terms with the fact that he is no more significant than the mosquito or the ant, he is doomed.' The coming of the ants highlights for me U.G.'s prophetic words. It shows me that all gods must eventually be destroyed and elemental life will prevail.

The aftershock of the morning incident has left us all rattled. I walk into the gorgeous garden trying to regain my equilibrium. A call from Pakistan gives me a taste of the real world. The country is going through political turmoil. Pervez Musharraf, the president, may be on his way out. By midday, I feel restless. I walk up to the tiny fridge in the corner and open it. There is just a golden box of Leonidas chocolates. I pull it out and greedily open the box. There are four chocolates in it. I offer them to Susan and Larry; they take one each. I dig into the box and holding those cold, creamy white chocolates, I turn to U.G. who is lying in front of me. 'Happy death day, U.G,' I wish him and pop the chocolates into my mouth.

At 2.33 p.m., we decide to hit the road and give U.G. a chance to slip away when no one is watching. Larry, Susan and I have come to the conclusion that U.G. will not go while any one of us is still in the room. It is Susan, who has experience with the sick and the dying, who put this idea in our minds.

Soon, Larry and Susan are in the garden, calling me out

to join them. Everything is still. I walk towards the door and turn. My master is clearly alive and still breathing. I bend down and touch his feet. They are coated with a white, ash-like dry skin. I feel my pulse throb but hardly any life in those toes with which I have such a friendship. I gaze at him affectionately and say, 'U.G., I'm going out so that you can go away. I want to thank you for all that you have done for me in case I don't find you here on my return.' Something in that very explosive silence tells me that my words have reached him, in some subliminal way. I bend down, kiss his feet and make a brave attempt to go out but can't. I am me; U.G. could walk away from things and never look back but I can't. So I turn back and look at him, inhaling the moment deeply; it is the only point in time I will retain with me and forever find sustenance from. I leave, feeling strangely like I am walking away yet am somehow standing next to U.G. My cellphone beeps, it is an SMS from Vishesh, my nephew: 'Please thank U.G. on my behalf. I have no words to express the importance of meeting him in my life.'

Susan, Larry and I wander the lazy deserted afternoon streets of Vallecrosia. We step into a departmental store, trying to figure out if any of us wants to buy anything. We realize that this is only one of our excuses to stay away from the villa. We then walk into a coffee bar to have a cappuccino. An Italian soap opera is playing on TV. The coffee bar is deserted. The lady who runs the place is happy to get some business at this unusual hour. Susan feels guilty at having abandoned U.G. I tell her that we are doing the right thing; we have chosen to do this. We soon find that in spite of all our attempts to stay away, we are heading back to the villa. We walk through the gate and all three of us do everything we can to keep ourselves from entering it. Mina runs up to me from nowhere and rubs her silken body against my leg. I bend down and ask her, 'Is my friend in or has he left?'

Larry, who is finding it impossible to stay away, decides to step in to check on the situation inside the cave. He stays away for quite some time. Then we hear him say, 'He has stopped breathing.' We try not to hurry into the room, pretending that we are in complete control and everything is normal. I find him exactly the way I had left him. His eyes are still open. I stare into them. 'He is gone,' I say. My old man has kept his pact. I was the only man he wanted to see in his final moment and that is how it happened. We prod Susan to feel his pulse. She does so. Then, turning to both of us, still holding his hand, she says with a look I'll never forget, 'Yes, he's gone.'

After the Death

22 March 2007, Vallecrosia

My mind, heart and body are placid and still. I step out into the afternoon sun and immediately call Ravi Thapar to inform him that U.G. has passed away. I also plead with him not to let the media in India get a whiff of this news. The funeral parlour in Bordighera is handling the cremation formalities for me. Mario, Sarito and Lucia, who have come to help within seconds of my informing them about U.G.'s demise, have accompanied me to this deserted funeral parlour to help me tide over possible bureaucratic roadblocks. The plan is soon made. A car will come and take him to the crematorium tomorrow at 2.30 p.m. I once again instruct everyone around me not to inform anyone that U.G. is dead. I'm doing this to make sure that no one gets the slightest idea of where he is to be cremated or where his ashes will finally rest. That's the way my old man wanted it and that's the way it is going to be.

Late in the evening, Susan, Larry and I have our first meal together in the kitchen. Susan, who prior to U.G.'s death did not want to leave the room for a second, does not want to even set foot in it now. 'His body has changed. The peace and absence of struggle that we felt after his passing away have left the room. Even you wouldn't want to go in there, Mahesh,' she says, still trying to cope with all that the three of us have been through in the last eight days.

'I would rather be called a fraud than a godman. Please do not put me in the category of the prophets; I am not an enlightened man.' This is the message that U.G. repeatedly kept hammering into everyone around him all his life. In spite of that, we superimposed on him our desire of what we wanted him to be for us. He always forced us to see that truth. The image that is seared in my brain is that of my god looking like a primordial beast, uttering not profundities but guttural, animal-like sounds and of his stone-like face being attacked by millions of black ants in the glory of the morning sunlight. Was this the 'last scene' that I was to witness? Did I come here to see the destruction and not the resurrection of the idea of my god? The story of the destruction of the idea called

U.G. underlines only one thing: he was mortal and not apart from ordinary men. U.G.'s story is the story of a man who refused to be god.

23 March 2007, Vallecrosia

The morning light wakes me up to a world without U.G. I am in great discomfort. A throbbing headache accompanied by a feeling of indescribable emptiness pulsates within me. I try my best to stay in bed but the momentum which has been driving me on pushes me out and sends me down the staircase. Susan is in the kitchen. She has had a bad night. We continue to talk about the significance, in our respective lives, of the eight days we have spent here in this villa. As I talk, sip coffee and chew on a piece of dry bread, I'm deeply aware that our silences are full with the knowledge that the old man is lying dead next door.

Mario and Sarito arrive. Mario informs me that Lucia has had a bad night. When I ask him why, he tells me that Lucia is uncomfortable with my suggestion that the stranger who cremates U.G. should be given the task of disposing of the ashes in some unknown location, thereby assuring by default that nobody, including myself, will know where they are. The reason I am unable to do this myself is that it will take at least six days for the cremation to take place; there is a queue before the fire. My staying on here would also put Lucia to further discomfort. She has already extended herself a great deal for us and I do not wish to take further advantage of her kindness. Moreover, we all really need to get on with our lives. That's the way U.G. would have wanted it.

I try to explain to an emotional Lucia that the idea of a poetic finale is not necessary to end the U.G. narrative. In spite of my animated persuasion, I find that she remains unconvinced. Therefore, I conspire with her. I entrust to her the task of scattering U.G.'s ashes in the Mediterranean Sea. My words have a magical effect on her. The cloud that has darkened her normally pleasant face lifts and she looks relieved. I whisper to her that this will now be our secret and no one should know of this arrangement. She assures me that she will honour the pact. My heart prompted me to do this because I felt that she too needed a sense of closure. After all, where in the world would U.G. have found a place like this to crawl into to die? Lucia so generously made that possible.

Larry, Susan and I get on the phone with Martin Butzberger of the Credit Suisse Bank, Gstaad. I want to get the entire will issue that U.G. had entrusted me with behind me as soon as I can. Larry and Susan are doing everything to help me cope with this unusual demand my old man has made of me, knowing very well that I have no idea of banking, wills or contracts. It is almost as if he's playing a practical joke with me from the beyond. Larry handles the business efficiently.

Without any warning, just like that, I announce to the group my decision to delegate the responsibility of scattering the ashes to Lucia. Lucia seems to be a bit taken aback by my sudden decision to make this private pact public. However, she is happy that this responsibility is being entrusted to her and that, by making my decision public, I'm acknowledging her integrity in this matter.

The men from the funeral parlour, some of whom look like burly goons straight out of an Italian gangster movie, arrive at 2.30 p.m. Wearing plastic gloves, they pick up U.G.'s corpse efficiently and place him in a glossy wooden box. Having done that, they turn towards me, sensing that I have an obvious emotional bond with the deceased. They want me to have the last look before they shut the lid on him forever. Larry and Susan have deliberately kept themselves out of this for reasons best known to them. I have my last look and the coffin's lid is shut. The box slides into a silver Mercedes hearse. My eyes fall on an ornate design of Jesus adorning the top of the car. The sight makes me smile. If U.G. could see that, he would leap out of the vehicle and run for his life. As the hearse door is about to shut, I pat the wooden coffin and say quietly, 'Goodbye, U.G.' The car drives off out of sight. I'm left with this feeling of emptiness and release, the kind of emotion that I was always left with when I used to see him off at airports. I can hear the gravel crunching under my feet as I turn to walk away. I pull out my cellphone to get on with the task of informing the world of the passing away of U.G. Krishnamurti. It is 3 p.m. and it's hot.

Mina the cat has strolled into U.G.'s cave. She's looking for someone who is not there. Mario, accompanied by Guha, is busy cleaning and dusting the cave in which U.G. breathed his last. I have to catch an early morning flight tomorrow from Nice. My daughter Shaheen calls to find out if I'm doing all right. She knows how badly the passing away of U.G. has affected me. Before I hang up, I say, 'You have to help me get these burning charcoals of memory which I have stored in my heart on to a computer screen,' referring to this diary which has more or less written itself. Larry and Susan take me out to dinner. The shared memories of the last eight days hold us close as we eat a giant-sized pizza together.

24 March 2007, Vallecrosia

It's 3.30 a.m. The silence seems to be burning my skin. I have packed my bags and am once again all set to hit the road. Mario and Guha will pick me up and then dump me at Nice airport shortly. Leaving this place with the realization that U.G. does not live here any more feels strange. Even if I walk away from this villa in Vallecrosia, a part of me will always live here till my dying day. While France sleeps, Mario and Guha drop me at the deserted Nice airport. 'The world without U.G. feels like a world with no gravity. When he was alive, no matter where we went, we felt his presence. He was our emotional centre and for me, my Kaaba and my Kashi,' I say to my friends as I hug them goodbye. As I step on to the tarmac to board the aircraft, the light around me changes. A heavy silence descends around us, deadening all sound. Then it begins to snow. It gets cold, very cold. A sudden, heartwarming memory, like a hot spring, surfaces in me. It was the first time I had been to Europe and Gstaad, in the late 1970s. It was snowing outside. 'Hey, snow!' I said.

'Stop the car,' said U.G. 'Go touch it.'

As I got down from the car and touched the snow I saw him watching me with the warmth of a mother watching her child play. I am overwhelmed by this memory.

28 March 2007, Mumbai

I call Lucia early in the morning to find out if she has immersed the ashes in the Mediterranean. 'I will do it this evening,' she says, sounding her usual efficient self. Today is the sixth day on this planet without U.G. Most of the people who have been very close to U.G. are doing just fine. This is the triumph of the master: he has not left cripples behind. Late that evening I call Lucia once again to find out if the job is done. The phone rings but there is no response. My heart tells me that she must be doing the job at this very moment. After a while, I call her again. She answers. Even before I can formulate my question, she says, 'Mahesh, I've just finished the task you assigned to me. I went in a sailing boat, far into the sea and as the wind blew, I let go of U.G.'s ashes.' There is great passion in her voice and I can hear the wind all around her. I can sense her deep fulfilment. As I bid Lucia goodbye and thank her for all that she has done, my mind imagines her standing in the boat, the wind blowing in strong gusts, and her letting go of U.G.'s ashes in a white, dusty stream behind her. My job is done. I have fulfilled the promise I made to my master. Even I do not know where his ashes finally travelled.

Epilogue

The door of the chamber opened and a thin, stooping, frail old man walked towards the courtyard of the mosque. He was dressed in a long, loose toga and a shawl was spread over his shoulders. He looked like the patriarch of some tribe. He was Hazrat Abu Bakr, the most outstanding figure of Islam after the Holy Prophet.

As he stood among the people, his furrowed face and tear-stained eyes betrayed the grief within him. In measured words, he said, 'Listen to me, ye people, those of you who worship Muhammad, know that he is dead, like any other mortal. But those of you who worship the God of Muhammad (PBUH), know that he is alive and will live forever.' A hushed silence fell on the assembly. They were stunned and bewildered with the poignancy of grief. Hazrat Abu Bakr wiped the tears from his eyes and recited the following verses from the Quran: 'Muhammad is but a messenger. Messengers of God have passed away before him. What if he dies or is killed? Will you turn back upon your heels?'

—From *Sidiq-i-Akbar Hazrat Abu Bakr*
by Masudul Hasan

The manner in which Shagufta Rafique, my writer, read out this passage to me in my office seared right through my frozen heart. The paper-thin dam within me which was holding back all the sorrow for the last one year since U.G. died crumbled and I began to weep uncontrollably. As tears coursed down my face, I began to see how vulnerable Abu Bakr must have felt without his prophet and how inadequate without the shield and insulation that his master's presence provided. I felt much the same although I had been trying to pretend to myself and to the world all these months that all was well. I was filled with overwhelming gratitude to Shagufta for reading this out to me because from this moment on, I would heal.

The months after U.G.'s death passed in a blur of fierce activity. The easiest thing for me to do was to create a firewall of frenzied movement for myself so that I would not have even a moment to hear the faintest whisper of that volcanic silence within me which was threatening to blow me apart. For a long time, I was like an open, festering wound and did not want anyone to touch me. I had stonewalled the hands that were reaching out to help. But little did I realize that the fire I had hoped to escape was coming from within me. And all this time, life, mundane, everyday, had been going on around me, apathetic to my anguish.

After U.G.'s death, the edifice called Mahesh crumbled and collapsed. Though I went through the motions of everyday life, concealing from the world my inner wasteland, there was no getting away from the fact that I had hit ground zero. Waves of the terror of death and extinction pounded the fortress of my consciousness. I would wake up in the middle of the night, mortified that I would be erased from this world. I had thought that the little world I had created for myself would just go on forever. The realization that I, too, like all living things, am just a guest on this planet and in my own body, terrified me. Death was no longer something that happened to someone else. With U.G.'s death, I was dying. What made matters worse for me was the fact that in his lifetime, U.G. had taken away all my gods, all my props which might have perhaps helped me now. I was shipwrecked, all alone, with nothing but myself to hold on to. Engulfed in this darkness, U.G.'s words came back to me: 'If the student cannot make it without the master, then there is nothing in him. You are the most courageous man I have met in my life. You have the courage to stand up and live life on your own.' I began to feel he was wrong. Perhaps my master's faith in me was misplaced.

Twentieth August 2008. It was raining flowers. They floated to the ground in fluffy white swirls and fell to the concrete. The sound permeated the crevices of my still mind. I lay awake in bed in the presidential suite of the Devigarh Palace in Udaipur, the city of dawn, where my daughter Pooja was shooting her film *Kajra Re*. I had come here just for a day to help Pooja out and having completed what was required of me, I was preparing to leave. I saw the moon; it was still in the sky, reluctant to leave its heavenly abode and make way for the flaming sun. The night cricket was here, too, singing its farewell song, even as the first sounds of the birds filled the air.

As I slipped my ageing body into my clothes, I discovered that the world outside was doing the same, changing her night garb for fresh clothes as it has been doing since the beginning of time. It is at this moment that day and night, and life and death, exist side by side in the same frame. Death, in fact, is the source of life. Enchanted by the falling flowers and the magical moment, I tiptoed towards the tree and stood under it, looking up. As I gazed at the canopy of flowers above me, I waited, filling myself with the fragrance of the tree in the honey-dipped silence. And then, as if bestowing me with a precious gift, the tree released a flower upon my person. It fell on my face softly, like an affectionate friend touching me on the cheek. Suddenly my sense of stone-like isolation melted away and I felt one with the tree and with everything around me. It dawned on me that I'm a part of the stream of life that changes continuously and relentlessly. The voice of my master erupted from within the very marrow of my bones, 'Mahesh will burn in this fire called U.G. and become a fire of his own and not an extension of this fire called U.G.' U.G. has lit the fire and left the room and it has been burning since. I know I can live up to the words of my master who told me, 'Don't let anything douse this fire or quench this thirst within you, Mahesh. Let it burn within you and char you to ashes.' Even though my house was on fire, I was not going to run out of it. I would stay inside, pour more gasoline, and turn to dust.